How to Go (Almost) Zero Waste

HOW TO GO *(Almost)* ZERO WASTE

Over 150 Steps to More Sustainable Living at Home, School, Work, and Beyond

Rebecca Grace Andrews, MA, MS

ROCKRIDGE
PRESS

This book is dedicated to healing the earth and to my daughter Helena, who first inspired my zero-waste journey and continues to inspire me daily to leave the earth a better place for future generations.

Interior and Cover Designer: Darren Samuel
Art Producer: Samantha Ulban
Editor: Vanessa Ta
Production Manager: Jose Olivera
Production Editor: Melissa Edeburn

All images used under license © iStock.

ISBN: Print 978-1-64739-868-2 | Ebook 978-1-64739-551-3

R0

Table of Contents

Introduction

Welcome!

About me: I've been working on sustainable living for 15 years. When I gave birth to my daughter, concern for her well-being prompted my research into food production, off-gassing of household items, toxins in diapers, and so on. As my daughter grew, so did my research and the changes we made.

Over the years, I went organic with our groceries, eliminated plastics, bought sustainable children's toys, planted gardens, grew and preserved food, composted, shopped at our local farmers' market, and sourced wardrobe basics from organic, U.S.–based manufacturers. For me, going (almost) zero waste has been easy because it's been a progressive process, one manageable step at a time. These changes left me feeling successful, positive, and eager to do more.

Eventually, I completed graduate degrees in herbal medicine and ecopsychology, the study of our relationship with the natural world and ways to live that are harmonious and sustainable. I offer health and wellness consultations on a variety of topics, work as a wellness professor, and write and speak on wellness and sustainability.

My family still ended up with far more trash at the curb than I was happy with, so more recently we've been trading out shampoo bottles for bars, buying reusable bags for bulk foods, and expanding our gardens.

About you: Maybe you're contemplating the path of sustainable living but aren't sure what it entails. Or maybe you're ready to commit to that path but don't know where to start or how to proceed. Or maybe you are already deep into a journey of sustainable living and want inspiration to take further steps.

I have good news for you: **You're in the right place.** This book presents baby steps and steps that require a larger investment of time and resources.

No matter where you are on the path to sustainable living, know that you are not alone. Think of each action as a drop of water going into a collective bucket. Once that bucket is full, notes Malcolm Gladwell in *The Tipping Point: How Little Things Can Make a Big Difference*, we hit a tipping point. Together, we can shift the culture and move toward a more sustainable way of living and relating to our earth home.

How to Use This Book

This book is designed to be used several ways.

» Work your way through slowly, trying out some steps here and there as you feel ready and able.

» Flip to a chapter that's of particular interest to you.

» Read the entire book before taking any steps.

Chapter 1 makes the case for zero waste. Chapter 2 presents 50 easy, under-$25 steps anyone can take. Chapters 3 through 10 focus on food and dining, personal care, housekeeping, work and school routines, celebrations, family life, conscious consumption, and community-wide efforts.

Each step in these chapters is labeled so you can tell at a glance how much money, time, and effort it might require, along with the impact it will have. Within each chapter, the steps are ordered by investment, from least expensive (under $25) to most expensive (grant funding or fundraising might be needed).

INVESTMENT:

Less than $25

$25 to $100

More than $100

Grant funding or fundraising might be needed

EFFORT:

Easy

Moderate

Difficult

TIME:

🕐
Less than two hours

🕐🕐
A good portion of a day or weekend

🕐🕐🕐
Many weeks, months, or even years

IMPACT*:

Small impacts

Moderate impacts

Major impacts

The impact factor reflects how the given step compares to other steps. For example, purchasing a reusable straw makes a small impact while purchasing reusable bags makes a major impact.

The most successful way to make changes is to start small. Take a few steps and allow yourself time to adjust to them. Don't beat yourself up when you stumble; that's part of the process. Just keep moving forward. You'll discover that each step you've taken has added up to some successful and major lifestyle changes.

Chapter One

What's the Case for Zero Waste?

You're about to embark on an exciting journey to benefit the planet. You've heard that zero waste is a good idea but might not know why.

Zero Waste International Alliance defines zero waste as "the conservation of all resources by means of responsible production, consumption, reuse, and recovery of products, packaging, and materials without burning and with no discharges to land, water, or air that threaten the environment or human health" (Zero Waste International Alliance 2018). **Waste is much more than the items we put out for our weekly trash pickup.** It also includes the waste produced in harvesting natural resources, in manufacturing items, and in disposing of or recycling materials. It includes waste that goes into our air, water, earth, and bodies. The goal of zero waste is to create a sustainable system wherein everything that we create goes back into the earth to nourish it, thereby creating no waste.

In this chapter, we'll look at just how much waste is going into our environment and in what ways, and we'll talk about the Three Rs: reduce, reuse, and recycle.

OUR HOME

Home sweet home ... The idea might conjure up images of family gatherings. It might evoke feelings of peace and comfort.

If your beloved home were threatened, you'd do everything in your power to save it. Right now, our earth home is threatened. It desperately needs a renovation before it becomes uninhabitable.

The World Counts website cited these statistics: In the first four months of 2020, more than 596 million tons of waste were deposited, 2 million people died from outdoor air pollution, and another 1 million died of indoor air pollution. Three billion tons of plastic were thrown into the ocean, and more than 1 million people died from lack of access to clean water. Much of the waste from developed nations is sent to the poor nations of Asia and Africa, a practice known as "toxic colonialism."

There is more carbon dioxide in our atmosphere than there has been in three million years, and 11 percent of the people on Earth are at high risk of climate-related weather catastrophes (Lindsey 2020).

Due to consumer demand for cheap goods in the United States and other rich nations, our world's resources are rapidly being depleted. Forest loss is responsible for the extinction of species, dirty air and water, a rise in carbon dioxide, and global climate change. Every minute, 36 football fields of trees are cut. Every day, about 14 Manhattan-sized rain forests are burned (Conservation International 2020). Eighty percent of this forest loss is due to increased conversion of lands for grazing to satisfy our demand for cheap meat in the West. There's some debate over whether animal agriculture or vehicle emissions create more greenhouse gases. Some sources state that animal agriculture alone accounts for at least 14.5 percent of our green-house gas emissions—more than every car, truck, plane, train, and ship on Earth (Food and Agriculture Organization of the United Nations n.d.; Carrington 2014; Andersen 2014). No matter how they're compared to vehicle emissions, agricultural emissions are too high. And every pound of ground beef you buy depletes 2,500 gallons of water (Andersen 2014).

Scientists warn that our earth home is in a state of emergency. According to The World Counts website, we have about 29 years left until we run out of food and all our systems collapse, but only 19 years until we run out of clean water.

We must do all we can now to save our home before it becomes uninhabitable.

The first step is to become mindfully aware of how we generate waste. Pretend that you're a scientist gathering facts in an unbiased and nonjudgmental manner. What can you learn about your own practices related to waste and sustainability?

Keep learning and working toward going (almost) zero waste to create a more sustainable lifestyle. You'll find plenty of ideas in the upcoming chapters. You can do a lot to preserve your home without feeling solely responsible for saving it. If we each do what we can, we'll collectively make a massive difference.

WASTE

The average American leaves behind 90,000 pounds of waste by the time they die (Brucker 2018). The World Counts tells us, "If you compare Earth's history to a calendar year then we (humans) have only existed for about 37 minutes—and we have used 33 percent of Earth's entire natural resources in the last 0.2 seconds!" We are simultaneously wasting resources and adding waste.

About 8 to 9 percent of the trash sent to U.S. landfills annually is rubber, leather, and textiles, meaning each American throws out about 81 pounds of clothing per year (Environmental Protection Agency 2014). More waste is pumped into the air and water to produce these clothes. Some $759 million was spent on cotton pesticides in the first four months of 2020. More than 5,000 gallons of water are required to produce just one cotton T-shirt and pair of jeans (The World Counts 2020; EcoWatch 2015).

The trash we throw out in the United States and Canada annually also includes 42 pounds of electronics per person (Platform for Accelerating the Circular Economy 2019).

Much of our waste doesn't even end up in a landfill. "The Great Pacific Garbage Patch," 617 thousand square miles of floating trash located between California and Japan, is the size of France and twice the size of Texas (*National Geographic* 2020; The World Counts 2020).

Our trash also ends up in our food and water. Twenty-five percent of fish sold in California markets had plastic particles in their guts, and upward of 90 percent of our tap water and bottled water contains microplastics (Kerlin 2015; Tapp Water 2019). Plastics are known carcinogens (cancer-causing substances) and/or hormone disruptors.

The U.S. Environmental Protection Agency (EPA) says that indoor air pollution is two to five times higher than outdoor air pollution for some contaminants (EPA 2018). The indoor air pollution is caused by chemical waste off-gassing from flame retardants, plastics, cleaning supplies, bath and body products, and scented items. The U.S. Food and Drug Administration does little to regulate chemical use; consequently, our personal hygiene and cleaning products contain known carcinogens, volatile organic compounds (VOCs), and phthalates, which are hormone disruptors that can affect the menstrual cycle, sexual development, and fertility (Environmental Working Group 2020; Food & Drug Administration n.d.). Many of these chemicals are banned in Europe.

In the United States, we waste about 150,000 tons of food daily, or one pound per person. World Vision reports that there are 815 million people worldwide going hungry and that our food waste could feed two billion (Huber 2017). We have neither an overpopulation issue nor a need for genetically modified foods to feed the hungry. What we have is mismanagement.

When we talk about going zero waste, we're not just talking about reducing the amount of trash you throw out weekly. We're talking about making sustainable choices that don't generate solid waste, plastic waste, air pollution waste, electronic waste, water pollution waste, food waste, clothing waste, and so on. If everyone consumed at the rate we do here in the West, we'd need five earths to support us (Downstream Project 2013).

This book will teach you how to take steps to make our earth home sustainable for all. Think of it as your new home improvement guide.

WHAT WE CAN DO

It's easy to get weighed down by such grim statistics. But we're going to focus on steps you can take to make a difference. Don't forget the analogy of the drops in the bucket. Together we are powerful.

If I resolve to carry only a reusable tote bag, I can personally reduce the number of plastic and paper bags by up to 22,000 (Reuse This Bag 2017). My choice results in fewer trees being cut, reduction in the millions of barrels of crude oil used annually to make plastic bags, less water waste, and less plastic trash. Imagine the collective impact when thousands of us choose reusable bags over plastic and paper.

Each step we take has profound and far-reaching impacts.

Reduce, Reuse, and Recycle

We begin by reducing the amount of trash we create in the first place, the amount of non-renewable resources we extract from the earth, the amount of water we dirty, and the amount of toxins we put into the air, water, and earth.

The next step is to reuse. When we consume, we can reuse by borrowing, sharing, buying used, and extending the life of products. Can you use something you already have? If not, no need to feel deprived: shop on Freecycle, Facebook Marketplace, Craigslist, eBay, or your local thrift or charity shop. If it's an item you'll only need to use once, maybe it's better to borrow it. Some neighborhoods have tool libraries, and some libraries lend electronics and other items. My neighbor and I have shared a car (when one was getting repaired), tools, and trash service.

Need clothes? Make arrangements with friends for an annual children's (or adults') clothing swap.

Finally, try to extend the life of items you buy. Mending can be beautiful and can even enhance an item of clothing. Think about upcycling (turning an unneeded item into something useful) instead of throwing things out. I save glass jars to store bulk food, herbs, and bath items. I cut old flannel pajamas into reusable rags. The plastic containers I occasionally buy can hold screws, screwdrivers, or garden seeds.

Recycling is the third option when reducing and reusing aren't possible. The EPA reports that recycling reduces water waste, conserves natural resources, cuts pollution, and saves energy, which in turn reduces the waste used in generating energy (EPA 2019). Right now, "a whopping 91 percent of plastic isn't recycled" (Parker 2019). Plastics, paper, batteries, and more can be recycled.

On Recycling

Many of us have gotten good at it, but the fact is that recycling isn't the best option.

Prior to 2018, seven million tons of recycling were shipped to China annually, where it was processed into new, cheap goods to sell to the West. The shipping and recycling processes created more waste through fuel for ships, building and powering recycling plants, and toxic byproducts of recycling that were contaminating communities. The Chinese government stopped accepting most foreign trash.

Trash companies used to make a profit by selling recycled goods. Now they have to pay big bucks to get them recycled. It's far cheaper to burn them or throw them in the landfill, which news reports tell us is happening to the majority of our recyclables, although accurate information is difficult to find.

Think of recycling as a last resort. Avoid buying things that will need to be recycled. You'll create far less waste that way.

Almost Zero Waste

Perhaps you've seen YouTube videos of people who fit their annual trash inside a canning jar. As inspiring as these zero-waste heroes may be, their lifestyle isn't realistic for most of us. That's why this book emphasizes two goals:

» Take whatever steps you can, remembering that the collective impact of each step is powerful.

» Aim for almost zero waste, not for perfection.

As you read this book, choose steps that feel doable to you. The key is to keep growing and to be the change you want to see.

Chapter Two

Baby Steps: Easy Swaps to Make Now

Whether you are just starting out on your zero-waste journey, pressed for time or money, or looking for something extra to add, this chapter is a great place to begin. The steps in it take only a few minutes and cost less than $25. Don't forget to look for sustainable items at your local discount big-box store, where I've found everything from reusable water and coffee containers to bamboo cleaning brushes to beeswax wraps. These items also make great wish-list choices for folks wanting to buy you a birthday or holiday gift.

Start by picking one or two things that feel easy. Take time to adjust to that change before taking more steps. This way, you'll create an upward spiral of success. If you are already doing some of the things in this chapter, congratulations. You're already on the path to (almost) zero waste.

1. **PURCHASE REUSABLE WATER BOTTLES.** By purchasing a reusable water bottle, you reduce the 315 plastic beverage bottles used annually per person in the United States—more than 100 billion bottles total. You'll cut into the 800 million tons of plastic that end up in our oceans annually, and you reduce the microplastics that last forever in our environment (Plastic Oceans 2014).

   Aim for bottles made from metal or glass to reduce the natural resources and production wastes associated with plastic manufacturing and plastic disposal. Consider getting one for work, one for home, and maybe one for the car, too.

2. **KEEP REUSABLE BAGS.** I immediately put them back in the car after I unload my purchases. For small purchases, bags aren't even necessary. I can easily carry a few items or tuck small things into my purse. Compact bags that fold into a neat little packet are great to stow in your backpack, purse, or glove box.

3. **BUY LOOSE PRODUCE INSTEAD OF PACKAGED.** When possible, choose produce that's not wrapped in plastic, in bags, or on Styrofoam trays. Instead of tucking your produce into plastic bags (including compostable ones, which create waste in manufacturing), purchase it with no bag at all, or buy ones made of reusable cotton. At home, your produce will last longer if it's not in a plastic bag, especially if you keep fruits and veggies separate (Sagon 2018).

4. **GIVE KIDS EXPERIENCES RATHER THAN PLASTIC AND BATTERY-OPERATED TOYS.** Great gifts are movie tickets, iTunes cards, a trip to a museum or arcade, a day at the lake, a membership to do something they love, or a leisurely day outdoors picnicking or exploring. Think outside the box, literally, when it comes to children's gifts. This reduces the trash from toy packaging as well as the plastic manufacturing and disposal waste from plastic toys that break easily.

5. **BUY REUSABLE STRAWS.** I drink just about everything with a metal straw, although bamboo and silicone straws are also good choices. (Unless you need plastic straws for medical reasons.) Metal

is sturdier than bamboo, and silicone contains some plastics, hence my preference for metal ones. With reusable straws, you reduce the 500 million used daily in the United States that contribute to much of the 800 billion pounds of plastic waste in our oceans (Parker 2018).

6. **BRING YOUR OWN SILVERWARE AND NAPKINS.** Keep these at work and/or in your car or purse. We have a little set in a holder with bamboo utensils, and a super cool spork on a keychain. You'll help reduce the 40 billion plastic utensils used annually in the United States (Tenenbaum 2019).

7. **PURCHASE A REUSABLE MUG FOR YOUR COFFEE OR TEA.** Reusable mugs come in every color and print imaginable; pick one you really love to make that warm beverage even more comforting. Styrofoam takes a million years to decompose, and paper depletes forests and has to be lined with fossil-fuel-derived plastics. A reusable mug will help reduce the 16 billion coffee cups thrown out annually (Helmer 2019).

8. **BUY IN BULK.** Mainstream grocery stores increasingly offer bulk dry foods, and pet stores will sell such supplies as cat litter that way. Bring your own containers or bags and reduce waste even further. Buying in bulk will cut food-packaging trash.

9. **REDUCE THE IMPACT OF YOUR PAPER GOODS.** Need disposable plates, cups, napkins, etc.? Choose paper, recycled if possible, instead of Styrofoam or plastic—or compostable and unbleached paper instead of the white glossy kind, if available.

10. **SHOP SECONDHAND.** Need a new dress for an office party, snow pants for your kids, or a waffle iron? Look for used first. Get to know thrift stores, eBay, Facebook Marketplace, Craigslist, and Freecycle. These are good ways to reduce waste.

11. **SKIP FABRIC SOFTENER AND DRYER SHEETS.** Both fabric softener and dryer sheets coat your clothing with toxic chemicals (Boyle and Geller 2016). There are safer, zero-waste, low-cost ways to get soft clothing free of static. Try wool dryer balls, hanging synthetics

to dry, or using a vinegar rinse in your washer. You'll reduce manufacturing and packaging waste and reduce the water and air pollution they cause.

12. **INSTALL A CLOTHESLINE OR DRYING RACK.** I call it a solar- and wind-powered dryer. It cost me under $20, saves me money, and as a bonus my clothes smell fresh and clean when they're hung out to dry in the open air. No yard, or tight on space? Consider hanging a collapsible drying rack in the shower or over your laundry area, even if you can't use it for all your laundry.

13. **TURN OFF THE WATER.** Turn off the water while brushing teeth and doing dishes. Wash dishes in less water. Reduce your shower by a minute or two. More than 80 percent of the world's wastewater ends up in our rivers, and this isn't just an issue in developing nations (Denchak 2018). By reducing your water use, you cut down on overloads to wastewater systems and the amount of sewage that goes into your local rivers.

14. **SKIP THE ANNUAL PHONE UPGRADE.** Your "old" cell phone will work well for years. When you do upgrade, buy the best phone possible so you can keep it longer. Must have that annual upgrade? Sign up for a plan that refurbishes or recycles your old phone. You'll help reduce the 40 million tons of electronic waste (e-waste) produced annually worldwide, and the toxins that electronics dump into landfills and water (The World Counts 2020).

15. **TURN YOUR HOT WATER HEATER DOWN TO 120 DEGREES FAHRENHEIT.** High hot water settings cost you an additional $36 to $61 annually when your hot water is off, and up to $400 extra for your actual water use. Save money and reduce your electric or gas use and the waste associated with energy production (Energy Saver 2020).

16. **ADJUST YOUR HEAT OR AC.** Adjusting your temperature by two to three degrees will save money and reduce energy waste. A three-degree temperature change could reduce your energy costs by 9 percent daily (Casey 2012). Away from home all day? Adjust the

temperature before you leave, or use a programmable thermostat. A 10- to 15-degree temperature change for eight hours of the day will reduce energy costs by 5 to 15 percent annually (Casey 2012).

17. **SKIP THE DRIVE-THROUGH AND IDENTIFY FIVE FAST MEALS YOU CAN MAKE AT HOME.** Meals like breakfast for dinner, pasta, a giant salad, a crockpot meal, sandwiches, and leftovers take little time to prepare. You'll save money, generate less waste, and eat healthier. Plan ahead so you have these things on hand on your busiest nights.

18. **GIVE THINGS AWAY.** Don't need something? Find someone in your circle who does. Host a clothing swap. Share power tools with neighbors. Pass on kids' hand-me-downs. Share trash service with your neighbor. Giving things away reduces the waste that ends up in landfills.

19. **BE SUSTAINABLE WITH NEW CLOTHING.** Try to skip or limit purchases that need dry cleaning. Choose natural fibers like cotton, linen, and wool over plastic-based synthetics. Many of the big organic companies have great sales. You'll be reducing the waste from manufacturing synthetic fibers or in non-organic cotton manufacturing.

20. **GET REUSABLE OR DECOMPOSABLE BAGGIES FOR LUNCHES.** Great replacements for plastic include beeswax wraps, silicone ziplock baggies, reusable metal, glass, or silicone containers, and paper sandwich bags.

Chapter Three

Food and Dining: Your Kitchen, Grocery Shopping, and Eating Out

I grew up in a community where food was a love language. Huge feasts of homemade goodness abounded, and you couldn't stop by someone's house without being invited to eat. To this day, I love good, flavorful, home-cooked meals.

In this chapter, you'll learn how to indulge your palate while increasing the safety of your food prep and lowering your environmental impact. By taking even a few of the steps in this chapter, you can help move our food production system toward more natural and sustainable methods. Voting with your dollars really counts.

21. PUT YOUR FOOD WASTE TO WORK.

Organic matter needs oxygen to compost back into soil. Scientists from Project Drawdown tell us that food scraps in landfills can't compost because of the lack of oxygen. Consequently they create methane gas, one of the more harmful climate-change emissions.

INVESTMENT:

EFFORT:

TIME:

IMPACT:

Use your vegetable trimmings to make soup stock.

If you have a yard, create a small compost pile. If it fits your family's budget, you can buy a special compost bin. No yard at all? See if your city has a zero-waste or composting program. Major cities across the United States and around the world have implemented compost programs; in some areas you can collect it in a countertop container and put it into a "green bin" with yard waste for your weekly trash pickup.

Consider an under-the-sink worm bucket. Worms eat the food scraps and produce beautiful composted garden soil for you.

22. EAT LOWER ON THE FOOD CHAIN.

According to some sources, animal agriculture is the No. 1 cause of harmful climate-change emissions worldwide, causing more emissions than every car, truck, plane, train, and ship combined. Exploitation of animals has resulted in Ebola, COVID-19, Swine Flu, and Avian Flu (Dalton 2020).

The documentary *Cowspiracy* states that 50 percent of the world's grains are grown for meat animals, and 82 percent of the world's starving children live in nations where grain is fed to animals to be eaten by people in wealthier nations (Andersen and Kuhn 2014).

The lower on the food chain and the more local you can eat, the more you cut down carbon emissions, reduce toxic waste in water and air, and minimize animal and human suffering.

INVESTMENT:

EFFORT:

TIME:

IMPACT:

Eating local, healthy, vegan meals is a great way to go zero waste. Check out documentaries such as *Game Changers*, *What the Health*, and *Cowspiracy* if you want to learn more.

Not everyone is ready to go vegan. One step in the right direction is to reduce your meat intake and use the extra money to buy from farmers where animals are raised on pasture rather than in factory farm feedlots.

Even if you eat local grass-fed and pasture-raised meat, reducing your intake is still important. Consider joining movements like Meatless Monday or Veganuary, an international movement to go vegan for the month of January.

23. PHASE OUT THE PLASTICS IN YOUR KITCHEN.

Advertisers are putting "BPA free" and "free of phthalates" on plastics now, which is a step in the right direction. The problem is that petroleum-derived items are seldom safe and never sustainable. Studies are finding that even the "safe" plastics—including BPA-free—contain potentially carcinogenic substances and other toxins that could affect the reproductive system (Saplakoglu 2018; Brandt-Rauf, et al. 2012). Not only will you protect your own health by using alternatives to plastic, you'll also be contributing to a reduction in the use of petroleum and the number of plastic items that ultimately end up in landfills.

INVESTMENT:	EFFORT:
	◗
TIME:	IMPACT:
◷	◔ ◔ ◔

Slowly phase out your plastics. Need a new cooking utensil? Purchase wood, metal, or bamboo. Looking for a blender? Pick the one with the glass pitcher. Need food storage? Opt for glass instead of plastic. Need plates for children? Look for bamboo, wood, or metal. Cleaning brushes? Get non-plastic ones.

Upcycle the glass jars from things like spaghetti sauce and use them to store food in the refrigerator or freezer (but leave a full one to two inches of empty space in the top of the jar to prevent bursting when freezing expands its contents), or for bulk items in the pantry. You'll end up with a growing collection of jars and uses for all of them.

24. CONSERVE WATER WHEN WASHING DISHES.

According to the Natural Resources Defense Council, handwashing supper dishes can use up to 27 gallons of water, whereas an Energy Star–certified dishwasher uses only three gallons per load (Postman 2016).

INVESTMENT:	EFFORT:
	◗
TIME:	IMPACT:
◷	◔

If you handwash, start with minimal water in the sink, rinse quickly, and turn it off as much as possible.

Don't forget to buy eco-friendly dish soap, especially for the dishwasher. Many dish soaps create toxic waste in water and even in the air. Toddlers have been hospitalized and some have even died from a lick of soap from the dishwasher. When that dishwasher door is open, the soap is at just the right height for curious toddlers and pets.

25. DO AWAY WITH PLASTIC TRASH BAGS BECAUSE THERE IS NO "AWAY."

The plastic bag that holds your trash is itself a piece of trash, adding to the landfill and taking decades or even centuries to decompose.

INVESTMENT:

EFFORT:

◖-◗

TIME:

🕐

IMPACT:

When my mom was a child in the 1950s, her family didn't use plastic garbage bags. They used a paper bag from the grocery store, lined it with old newspaper from the week before to soak up any liquids, and carefully drained any liquids before trashing items.

Buy compostable plastic bags.

(If you can reduce, reuse, recycle, and compost, you probably won't have much trash anyway.)

26. KEEP REUSABLE RAGS.

Earlier I mentioned the amount of textile waste that goes into landfills annually, and the negative consequences of that waste.

INVESTMENT:

EFFORT:

◖

TIME:

🕐

IMPACT:

Cut your old flannel pajama pants or T-shirts into rags as an alternative to paper towels. Simply cut them into rag shapes, or sew them into more durable, double-thick rags. Rinse them out and throw them in the laundry for reuse later.

Save paper towels or wipes for really gross animal or kid messes (you know the kind). There's no reason you can't use cloth on those, too, but if that's all you're using paper for, you've made a huge step in the right direction.

If you do buy paper towels, opt for ones made from recycled paper and in recyclable plastic wrap.

27. BULK UP.

Buying in bulk eliminates packaging, especially if the store allows you to bring your own container. At most stores that carry bulk, customer service will weigh your clean containers and put a weight sticker on them. The weight of the container is then deducted from the total at checkout. Bulk items also typically cost less, since there's less manufacturing cost from packaging.

INVESTMENT:

EFFORT:

TIME:

IMPACT:

Health food stores and some larger grocery stores sell pasta, grains, granola, nuts, crackers, dried fruit, and more in bulk bins.

The hardest part of buying in bulk is usually remembering your reusable containers. So as soon as you have unpacked and put away groceries, place some empty jars in your reusable bags and run them out to the car so you have them handy for the next time.

Can't find bulk food items? Look for store brands to save money or shop online from zero-waste retailers such as Zero Waste Cartel, Chagrin Valley, Azure Standard, and Package Free Shop.

28. REDUCE PACKAGING.

Loose produce or produce in a bag? It's easier to grab the five-pound bag of potatoes, apples, or onions and go, but it will add another piece of plastic waste to our landfills.

INVESTMENT:

EFFORT:

◑-◯

TIME:

🕐

IMPACT:

Whenever possible, opt for produce without packaging.

Shopping for ingredients, rather than full packaged meals, also reduces packaging. Meal planning and making extras to freeze staves off the need to buy things that come in plastic and cardboard.

Some folks enjoy having a meal prep party with friends. Each family makes one huge dish to feed five families, and then everyone trades meals so that each family ends up with five meals for the freezer.

29. BYO TO REPLACE DISPOSABLES WHEN DINING OUT.

By bringing your own, you save water and reduce plastic production and consumption. You help reduce the 40 billion plastic utensils that enter US landfills annually. Getting takeout? Tell the restaurant, "Hold the silverware and napkins; I brought my own."

INVESTMENT:

EFFORT:

◑-◯

TIME:

🕐

IMPACT:

Keep reusable silverware, a water bottle and/or coffee mug, and cloth napkins in your vehicle, backpack, or handbag, as mentioned in chapter 2. Keep a set at work, too, to replace disposables from fast food and takeout places.

Opt for metal or bamboo utensils and water bottles rather than plastic.

To be extra eco, look for linen, hemp, or organic cotton napkins. Conventional cotton uses huge amounts of water and pesticides in production.

If you're in a sit-down restaurant, you can usually use your own container to pack up leftovers. When a local café told my friend that regulations prohibited them from taking customer containers into their kitchen, my friend asked if they'd purchase canning jars and charge him $1 extra (the cost of the canning jar). The restaurant was open to this option and diners were happy to pay the extra $1 that resulted in a new glass storage container for them to use at home. Most important, plastic and Styrofoam container consumption was greatly reduced.

30. DOWNLOAD AN APP.

In this day and age, apps put the info we want literally at our fingertips. Whether you travel frequently or just want to keep tabs on healthy food in your hometown, these apps will have you covered.

INVESTMENT:

EFFORT:

TIME:

IMPACT:

Local Eats provides a list of all locally owned cafés and restaurants; no chains are included.

Falling Fruit identifies local fruit trees for foraging.

Farmstand connects you with local farmers' markets.

HappyCow and *Clean Plates* let you search for restaurants with vegetarian, vegan, kosher, gluten-free, or organic options.

Seasons and *What's Fresh* tell you what produce is in season in your region at any given time.

ShopNoGMO and the *Non-GMO Project Shopping Guide* help you avoid GMOs while doing your grocery run.

31. SUPPORT YOUR LOCAL FARMERS.

Shopping from farmers keeps money in the local economy, supports sustainable farms, and gets you the most delicious seasonal food imaginable. It also reduces the amount of gasoline needed to truck food to you. The average meal travels 1,500 miles to your table. A local diet sources foods from a 100-mile radius.

INVESTMENT:

EFFORT:

TIME:

IMPACT:

Check out localharvest.org to get started.

Get to know your local farmers through farmers' markets and Community Supported Agriculture (CSA) programs.

When I had more time than money, I bartered some work on a farm for boxes of tomatoes to make sauce. I also brought home many pounds of free beets that had little nibbles from pests in them. The farmers can't sell them like that, even though they're safe to eat. I cut off the nibbled sections and canned a delicious beet chutney that we enjoyed all winter long.

32. GO ORGANIC.

Organic foods are grown without toxic herbicides, pesticides, and fungicides. Buying organic helps protect farmers—especially the migrant workers who lack rights—and helps keep toxic waste out of our air, water, and earth. Ideally, we would all purchase 100 percent organic, but that's not realistic for most folks.

INVESTMENT:

EFFORT:

TIME:

IMPACT:

Familiarize yourself with the annual Dirty Dozen and Clean 15 lists from the Environmental Working Group (EWG) so you know which items are the most contaminated and should be purchased organic (Environmental Working Group 2020).

Keep in mind that toxins accumulate in fats, so dairy, eggs, and meat should always be purchased organic when possible (Donley 2016).

If you want to know about your local farmers' practices, ask questions and visit their farms to see for yourself. Any farm worth buying from will be transparent, answer questions, and welcome a visit.

When you shop for organic foods, it's important to understand the labeling (Global Organics n.d.). By understanding these labels, you can purchase items that were produced in ways that are healthier for the earth, healthier for workers, healthier for animals, and ultimately healthier for you. Do what works for your family; each step you take will reduce waste.

USDA Organic: all ingredients are organic. Some states have their own certifications such as California Certified Organic Farmers (CCOF) and Oregon Tilth.

Organic: 95 percent of its ingredients are organic.

Made with organic ingredients: 70 percent of its ingredients are organic.

Humane: This is a nebulous idea with no exact definitions or legal requirements.

Certified Humane®: This organization certifies farms based on various practices, some of which are outlined further below.

Cage-free: Birds are not in cages, but they're crowded into a barn in unhealthy and inhumane conditions, usually less than one square foot per bird.

Free-range: Birds are crowded in a barn with a small area of access to the outdoors that they may or may not be able to find. In fact, a window that they can stick their head out counts as "free range." Certified Humane® free-range birds must have two square feet of space per bird and be outside six hours per day.

Grass-fed: Animals are out on pasture in warmer weather and eat hay in winter.

Natural: The item cannot contain artificial ingredients and must be minimally processed, but it may not be grown or raised in natural ways.

Pasture-raised: Animals are out on pasture. If your meat is Certified Humane® and labeled pasture-raised, this means no more than 1,000 birds per 2.5 acres (Certified Humane 2014).

Certified naturally grown: This is an alternative to expensive USDA organic certifications. Many smaller farmers will use this because they can't afford organic certification or because they feel the standards are higher.

33. SKIP THE GMOS.

There's a lot of confusion about the safety of genetically modified organisms (GMOs) and what genetic modification (GM) is. Don't confuse hybridization with GM. Think of hybridization as when a black dog and white dog have black and white puppies. Think of GM as putting shark genes into your puppy so it will like water better. One process is natural and one is not.

The majority of the world's nations and scientists ban or in some way regulate genetically modified foods based on scientific studies showing their potential harm (Walia 2014; Bello 2013; Sustainable Pulse 2015). Studies have shown that GM crops ultimately end up using more toxic chemicals, even though the goal was for them to use less (Non-GMO Project 2016). By avoiding GMOs you put less toxic chemical waste into our environment and vote with your dollars for more sustainable farming practices. If the studies on the potential harm of GMOs are true, then you're protecting your health, as well.

INVESTMENT:

EFFORT:

TIME:

IMPACT:

Educate yourself about the crops that are currently GM. Biotech company International Service for the Acquisition of Agri-biotech Applications (ISAAA) has a list of all the crops that are currently GM: isaaa.org/gmapprovaldatabase/cropslist/default.asp

If you buy organic you automatically avoid GMOs.

Look for the black-and-white butterfly logo from the Non-GMO Project. Their website, NonGMOProject.org, is an excellent resource for GMO information as well.

34. SKIP THE NONSTICK PAN.

All Teflon pans are coated with a proprietary chemical mixture. New regulations ordered the elimination of two highly toxic materials found in the original Teflon pans, but today the pans are still allowed to contain toxic per- and polyfluoroalkyl substances (PFAS). More than 200 scientists from around the world have united to speak out against the use of PFAS. They published an article in a peer-reviewed scientific journal calling for PFAS to be regulated, citing in animal studies the harm they have caused and the amount of toxic waste they put into the environment (Blum, et al. 2015). So while PFAS are currently allowed in Teflon, it's debatable whether they're really safe or are still putting toxic waste into the environment.

INVESTMENT:

EFFORT:

TIME:

IMPACT:

Ceramic is a much safer alternative and gives you that great nonstick surface. The downside to ceramic? It's not biodegradable—pieces of ceramic and ceramic dust can be found in the environment dating back 10,000 years—but at least ceramics don't harm the environment the way microplastics and Teflon chemicals do (Ceramics 2020).

My personal favorite cookware is cast iron, even though it's not quite as slick as Teflon or ceramic. Cast iron pans can last for a lifetime and much longer, often being passed down among family members. When they are well seasoned, foods won't stick as much as you think they will.

Learn how to care for cast iron, and don't be afraid to buy an old, rusty, dirty one at a sale. They can be cleaned up and seasoned to be used again, though it's a bit of a difficult process. All my cast iron has been purchased on the cheap from garage sales.

If you're not looking for a nonstick surface, stainless steel pots are great. Avoid materials like copper and aluminum, which can leach into food.

35. INVEST IN REUSABLE FOOD COVERS.

It can be difficult to imagine what our grandparents used before plastic wrap, aluminum foil, and plastic baggies, but reusable food wraps keep all sorts of trash out of the environment.

INVESTMENT:

EFFORT:

TIME:

IMPACT:

Use silicone lids that stretch to fit over various-sized dishes and pans. My mom bought me a set after being horrified by my habit of just stuffing things in the fridge with no lids due to my aversion to plastic and aluminum wraps.

Beeswax-coated cotton wraps are also popular; they can be found at big-box discount stores such as TJ Maxx and HomeGoods.

Bread and vegetables can be wrapped in cotton or linen bags, and all sorts of options exist for packing sandwiches and other light foods (see chapter 6).

36. PURCHASE SAFETY-CERTIFIED KITCHEN CLEANERS OR MAKE YOUR OWN.

The Environmental Working Group has found that many cleaning products, including so-called green or natural/organic ones, contain chemicals known to cause asthma, respiratory issues, and allergies; reproductive issues including birth defects; and cancer, burns, and poisonings (Environmental Working Group 2020). We spray these cleaners right onto surfaces we later prepare food on or eat from.

No oversight agency monitors the safety of our cleaning products (Scheer and Moss 2011). Furthermore, there's no legal requirement for a company to list all the ingredients in a cleaning product, so you might be seeing a partial list.

By using alternative products, you reduce the number of chemicals in production, vote with your dollars for safer options, reduce air and water pollution, and if you make your own, reduce plastic packaging.

INVESTMENT:
–

EFFORT:

TIME:

IMPACT:

Vinegar sprays and baking soda are very effective, natural alternatives. I clean much of my kitchen with a straight vinegar spray, sometimes adding in a bit of baking soda.

If you prefer to purchase something, the EWG offers multiple options for healthier cleaners.

37. DINE LOCAL.

By eating local, you reduce the emissions from shipping foods long distances and keep money in your local economy. (You can choose to eat local at home, too.)

INVESTMENT:
–

EFFORT:

TIME:

IMPACT:

Farm-to-table restaurants try to source all or most of their food from within a 100-mile radius, usually purchasing directly from farms. Meals are typically fresh and delicious. Google "farm to table" and your city or town's name and see what you find.

No farm to table? Patronize locally owned mom-and-pop restaurants rather than national chains. The food and service are often better, and money stays in the local economy. These restaurants are often open to sourcing food locally if you connect them with local farmers. See chapter 10 for more ideas.

38. PICK YOUR OWN.

By picking your own fruits and vegetables, if local farms offer this opportunity, you create earth-loving annual traditions that reduce fossil fuel waste from shipping, cut down on food manufacturing and packaging waste, and create delicious experiences to enjoy all year long.

INVESTMENT:
–

EFFORT:

TIME:

IMPACT:

Look for a farm that uses organic, no-spray, or integrative pest management (IPM), all of which reduce environmental toxic waste. Carpool to the farm with friends to reduce use of fossil fuels—plus, the more the merrier, right? Don't forget to bring your own containers, and save them for the following year.

Follow your picking with a get-together with family and/or friends to make strawberry shortcakes or apple pie or carve pumpkins, for example. If you have kids, these sorts of outings and food traditions are great ways to celebrate the seasons and foster a love for the earth.

In both urban and rural areas, foraging might also be an option. My daughter and I have an annual tradition of making wild mountain apple pie from apples we gather from century-old trees scattered around our region. We also know of several fields of wild berries free for the picking. Connect with local herbalists, foragers, farmers, or friends who know where free, legal spots exist and can teach you to identify wild edibles.

Consider picking enough to freeze, can, or make jam so you can enjoy your harvest all year long. Reusing your BPA-free freezer bags will further reduce your waste.

39. GROW YOUR OWN.

Whether it's in a pot in a sunny window, a 4' x 4' raised bed, an urban community garden plot, or a permaculture landscape, fresh food is a joy to produce. Growing your own produce is a great way to go organic on the cheap, protect our environment, reduce petroleum use for packaging and shipping, and eat the freshest in-season foods.

INVESTMENT:
—

EFFORT:
◖ - ◖

TIME:
◔ - ◔◔◔

IMPACT:
◔

Google "join a community garden" or "community gardens near me" to find local resources.

YouTube and farm and garden websites have great resources to get you started at home. For example, Soul Fire Farm hosts a weekly session, *Ask a Sistah Farmer*, a free online show "to support people who want to grow their own food and medicine for self-reliance and community resilience" (Soul Fire Farm 2020).

It's amazing how much you can grow in a little 4' x 4' box garden. I get untreated pine from the hardware store, cut each eight-foot board in half so it's four feet, and nail (difficult) or screw (easy) the pieces together to make a square. Contact your local cooperative extension office to find out where you can get a mix of topsoil and compost for your box.

40. SHARE SOME CSA GOODNESS.

Community-supported agriculture (CSA) is a tremendous way to get fresh, local food while helping a small family farm. You pay a set fee to receive a specific amount of fresh produce throughout the growing season. Each week you pick up your box of goods from the farm or a location near your home or have it delivered right to your door. Some CSAs provide fresh produce specifically to areas called food deserts (where access to affordable and nutritious food is extremely limited or nonexistent).

INVESTMENT:

EFFORT:

TIME:

IMPACT:

Find your local CSAs by checking localharvest.org or asking around at a farmers' market.

Find a CSA that works with your budget. In the original CSA model, consumers pay before the actual growing season as a way to provide farmers with a guaranteed income for planting. Some CSAs now allow a weekly payment plan. This strategy works especially well for those who are on a tight budget or want to use their Supplemental Nutrition Assistance Program (SNAP) benefits. Some CSAs also offer an income-based sliding fee.

Chapter Four

Personal Care: Bathroom and Body Care Products

Have you ever checked to see whether your favorite personal care products are safe for you and the earth? You might be surprised to learn some of the products you thought were benign are actually causing you harm. Fortunately, a world of alternative personal care products exists. Start with one or two changes that feel manageable.

41. USE THE EWG HEALTHY LIVING APP TO CHECK PRODUCT SAFETY FOR HAIR CARE, COSMETICS, SHAVING, THE BATH, AND MORE.

People use 6 to 12 body products daily. Does the FDA guarantee the safety of these personal care products? No.

The FDA requires companies to test their ingredients, but it does not check to see if those safety tests were conducted or approve the chemicals used in products (U.S. Food & Drug Administration n.d.). In fact, the United States allows about 1,000 chemical ingredients that were banned by the European Union (Isaacs-Thomas 2019). To further complicate issues, labels aren't required to disclose all ingredients; for example, "fragrance" can be a combination of 3,100-plus chemicals (Frack and Sutton 2010).

Sunscreen, shampoo, and shaving cream use PFAS, which hide behind many names on ingredient lists (Formuzis 2018). Our bath and body products also contain known phthalates (hormone disruptors that cause issues with sexual development, the menstrual cycle, and fertility) and carcinogens (Naveed 2014). Our skin is a spongelike surface; what goes on the skin goes into the body's fat and blood and washes down the drain and into our wastewater.

Buying "natural" or "hypoallergenic" personal care products doesn't guarantee safety, either, because there are no legal requirements for using these words on a product. They're basically just marketing terms (Fasanella 2017; Ahmed 2018).

INVESTMENT:

EFFORT:

TIME:

IMPACT:

Check the EWG's Skin Deep Database before you buy bath and body products. Download the EWG Healthy Living app on your phone and instantly check the safety of about 120,000 body products and foods.

The EWG database will let you check out the safety of shampoo and conditioner, hair dyes, makeup, lotions, sunscreen, moisturizer, bubble bath, nail polish, and more. You'll be reducing the amount of toxic waste that ends up in our bodies, our air, and our water.

When you're shopping for new products, don't forget to look for the leaping bunny symbol. This symbol indicates that the product was not tested on animals, furthering environmental safety. Animal testing involves exposing animals to high concentrations of toxic chemicals and diseases and then disposing of their bodies, leaving the chemicals and diseases behind. No animal testing = less waste and more environmental safety.

42. RAISE THE BAR WITH SUSTAINABLE SOAPS.

The EWG app will show you which toxic chemicals are in common soaps. Using sustainable soaps eliminates packaging as well as toxic waste in our water and air, and on our bodies.

INVESTMENT:

EFFORT:

TIME:

IMPACT:

Switch out your packaged body wash and liquid soaps for bar soaps. Health food stores have great options with many scents (or no scent).

Check that the product is scented with herbs and essential oils rather than with chemical fragrance.

If you love liquid soaps, look for recipes to make your own. (My mom makes foam soap and simply refills her containers.) Some stores also offer the option to refill your liquid soaps from bulk.

43. PROTECT YOUR SKIN WITHOUT POISONING IT.

Ever step into a pool or lake and see a slight film across the top of the water? That's from sunscreen that washes off and pollutes the water. Many sunscreens contain known toxins to our reproductive systems that show up quickly, after application, in blood and breast milk (Bedosky 2019; Environmental Working Group 2020). We're trying to protect ourselves from one disease while potentially causing others.

INVESTMENT:

EFFORT:

TIME:

IMPACT:

Naturally, it's important to protect our skin. Holistic doctors recommend no more than 15 minutes of sun bathing to absorb vitamin D. Start with fewer minutes if you have pale skin.

Use a safer sunscreen, approved by the Environmental Working Group. You'll pay more for a safe one, but your long-term health is worth it. Right now, the only sunscreen ingredients that the FDA has legally given "generally recognized as safe" (GRAS) status are zinc oxide and titanium oxide (Bedosky 2019; Environmental Working Group 2020). Using safe sunscreens protects us and our water from toxic waste in both production and use.

44. GO FOR ZERO-WASTE MINTY FRESHNESS.

Mouthwash has become a routine part of oral hygiene, but most mouthwash comes in a plastic container. The EWG rates some of the most popular mouthwash brands only "fair" in terms of safety. Replacing your mouthwash routine with a more sustainable one means better oral health, less toxic chemical waste, and reduction of our reliance on plastics.

INVESTMENT:

EFFORT:

TIME:

IMPACT:

Find recipes to make your own mouthwash.

Shop for mouthwash in a sustainable container from online zero-waste retailers.

Trade the mouthwash for oil pulling with sesame or coconut oil. (Add a couple drops of pure mint extract or one drop of peppermint essential oil to a spoonful of coconut oil if you just have to have that mint flavor.) Oil pulling means swishing the oil around in your mouth and pulling it between the teeth for 5 to 20 minutes before spitting it into the trash and brushing your teeth again. A 2017 study found oil pulling quite effective at reducing oral bacteria, plaque, and gingivitis (Naseem, et al. 2020).

45. FIND A NEW SIGNATURE SCENT.

It really gets into personal space here talking about how you smell. Remember that "fragrance" is a proprietary blend of thousands of chemicals, many of which are known toxins and can cause reproductive damage (Environmental Working Group, 2020).

INVESTMENT:

EFFORT:

TIME:

IMPACT:

Nobody is telling you to dab yourself with patchouli or lavender, unless you like them. There are some sophisticated all-natural scents on the market today. Sage Goddess makes fragrances suitable across the gender spectrum, with countless options and sample sizes available.

Your trusty EWG app can recommend other healthy fragrances. Find a signature scent that represents the new, more-eco you. You'll be reducing chemical production and air pollution along the way.

46. REDUCE THE AMOUNT OF WATER YOU USE.

Unless you have a septic system, all the water from your washer, toilet, and sink ends up as wastewater. Theoretically, it goes to a treatment plant where it's cleaned and pumped back into our pipes for reuse, but much of it ends up contaminating our environment. Municipalities often end up with more wastewater than they can handle, and many US cities dump excess sewage right into our rivers.

About 860 billion gallons of wastewater end up in our rivers annually, often making people sick in the process (American Rivers n.d.). This is enough sewage to flood the entire state of Pennsylvania ankle deep.

INVESTMENT:

EFFORT:

TIME:

IMPACT:

Install a low-flow showerhead.

Use a low-flush toilet.

Reduce the length of your showers.

Turn off water when not in use.

Use Energy Star appliances; all reduce wastewater production.

47. TAKE A BITE OUT OF PLASTIC POLLUTION WHILE PROTECTING YOUR PEARLY WHITES.

A billion toothbrushes are thrown away in the United States annually, creating 50 million tons of plastic waste in our landfills, much of which ends up in streams, rivers, and oceans (Erskine 2020). Remember, plastic never decomposes; it only breaks down to microplastics that end up in our food and water. Unless you're a small child, you're not about to consider not brushing your teeth. What's a person to do?

INVESTMENT:	EFFORT:

TIME: IMPACT:

Buy a toothbrush made from recycled plastic that's recyclable after use.

An even better option is to buy a bamboo toothbrush. The bamboo felt weird in my mouth after using a smooth plastic one for four-plus decades, but it feels good to know that I'm not putting plastics into my mouth or the environment.

You can find more sustainable toothbrushes at your local health food store, at zero-waste online retailers, and even on Amazon. Bonus points if you find one with plant-based bristles. Then your entire toothbrush can be composted. Within three to six months it will be nothing but soil.

48. SKIP THE TOOTHPASTE TUBES.

Did you know that more than a billion toothpaste tubes end up in landfills annually? If we stacked them up, that would be the equivalent of 50 Empire State Buildings (Bedwell 2019).

INVESTMENT: EFFORT:

TIME: IMPACT:

Some companies are beginning to make recyclable toothpaste tubes, which is an excellent step, but you'll remember from chapter 1 that there are serious issues with recycling.

Another option is to buy toothpaste tablets from online zero-waste retailers. These look like little mints and dissolve in the mouth as you brush your teeth. They come in compostable or recycled paper packages and can be stored in reusable containers.

If you have pets, look for brands without xylitol. While xylitol is harmless to humans and good for our teeth, it's actually highly toxic to animals. My favorite brand is Unpaste Toothpaste Tablets simply because they're one of the few without xylitol.

You'll also find multiple recipes online for homemade tooth powders. These are super easy to make and very inexpensive, and reportedly work quite well.

49. GO ZERO WASTE WITH YOUR SHAVING CREAM.

In addition to the chemicals used in most shaving creams or foams, the production and disposal of shaving cream packages presents many waste problems.

INVESTMENT:

EFFORT:

TIME:

IMPACT:

Consider going the old-fashioned route with bar soap, or order bar shaving cream from an online zero-waste retailer.

Check your favorite products on the EWG app.

50. CUT THE STINK WITHOUT STINKY PACKAGING.

It can be difficult to find an eco-friendly deodorant that you really love, so have patience with this one. Many users report trying multiple brands or recipes before finding one that works well.

INVESTMENT:

EFFORT:

TIME:

IMPACT:

Check the EWG website for sustainable options.

Target and other stores sell deodorant in cardboard rather than plastic.

You can find recipes online to make your own, and with the right combination of ingredients, it couldn't be easier.

51. GET FLOSSING.

Most dental floss is problematic simply because it's made from plastic. And it's often coated with toxic PFAS to help it slide more easily between the teeth (Harvard 2019). By choosing a healthier dental floss, you can also save thousands of small animals from getting tangled in its strings, keep plastics out of the environment, and protect your own health.

INVESTMENT: EFFORT:

TIME: IMPACT:

Health food stores and zero-waste online retailers sell dental floss made of biodegradable materials, with no PFAS, sold in biodegradable or refillable glass containers.

You can also find silk floss or floss coated with beeswax, or use a water pick for more sustainable solutions.

52. PURIFY YOUR BATHROOM AIR.

Bathrooms can get rather stinky. It's habit for many of us to use air freshener, masking the smell with an aerosol or plug-in of chemical sweetness. By avoiding those options, you keep chemical production lower, reduce use of plastics and metals, and reduce air pollution from VOCs and carbon.

INVESTMENT:

EFFORT:

TIME:

IMPACT:

Check EWG for non-toxic air fresheners.

Or make your own air freshener. Essential oil diffusers or homemade herbal potpourri with essential oils help mask smells and make air more fragrant. Just remember to check for essential oil safety if you have small children, animals, or people with lung or liver issues.

Finally, don't forget that one of the easiest ways to kill the stink is to light a match.

53. MAKE SURE YOUR BATHROOM IS TRULY CLEAN, NOT JUST CHEMICAL-COATED.

By opting for green clean, you reduce the number of plastic containers produced and trashed and cut down the chemical waste contaminating our environment.

INVESTMENT:

EFFORT:

TIME:

IMPACT:

Check your favorite cleaners in the EWG database. Cleaners aren't regulated and contain all sorts of harmful chemicals. How do your favorites rate for safety?

If there's one place in our homes we want squeaky clean, it's the bathroom. Don't get sold on the idea that we need a separate cleaner for every surface. One good all-purpose cleaner is often sufficient. Make your own or choose an eco-friendly brand that comes in a recyclable container and rates well in the EWG database.

In addition to an all-purpose cleaner, my first choice for a scouring cleaner is baking soda, which I can purchase in bulk in a canning jar: a truly zero-waste option. Also, Bon Ami's gentle powder cleaner scours without scratching. It is perfect for toilets and tubs, is biodegradable, and comes in a biodegradable package.

Many people enjoy making their own cleaners with apple cider vinegar, lemon, baking soda, or essential oils as disinfectants. Studies show that all these items have various cleaning and/or antibacterial properties. Look for reliable recipes online and check out the cleaning ingredients via studies on Google Scholar. Remember, essential oils are not always safe for use around infants, toddlers, and pets. While they are natural, they are highly concentrated chemicals that can cause respiratory problems or harm the liver if used incorrectly.

54. DON'T SHOWER IN A COCKTAIL OF CHEMICALS.

We love our daily shower, but how clean are we getting if our lungs are being bathed in a chemical cocktail? Vinyl shower curtains and bath mats are infamous for off-gassing due to the polyvinyl chloride (PVC) in them. PVC contains VOCs, phthalates (hormone disruptors, aka reproductive toxins), and carcinogens (Occupational Health & Safety 2018). Remember: toxic off-gassing is not just a health issue, it's also a waste concern.

INVESTMENT:

EFFORT:

TIME:

IMPACT:

The easiest option for most people is to opt for a shower curtain made of natural fibers and a polyester liner that can be washed and reused for a lengthy period. Of course, polyester is still a plastic and won't break down in a landfill, and other options can be pricey, although you can find them on sale.

If you're able to invest money for a longer-term and more sustainable solution, a glass shower door is a great option. Alternately, Rawganique, an online retailer, sells hemp shower curtains that can be waterproofed with a wax they sell.

While you're greening the bathroom, skip the plastic trash bucket and opt for metal or bamboo. Look for bamboo, wood, metal, or glass for other bathroom storage, and opt for towels made of natural fibers (organic if possible) instead of plastic-based microfibers.

55. MAKE YOUR HAIR GREEN (NOT LITERALLY).

Any option in this step gets you a great hair-care product while reducing plastic waste and exposure to toxic fragrances.

INVESTMENT:	EFFORT:
–	
TIME:	IMPACT:

Switch to shampoo and conditioner that come in a bar, like soap. The bars are pricey compared to a bottle of shampoo, but last for several months. I like Chagrin Valley brand because they offer products for all hair types and I can purchase sample sizes. The bars don't lather up quite as much as typical shampoos and my hair felt a bit gritty as I rinsed, but it was very soft when it dried.

Zero Waste Cartel is another favorite online store for bar shampoos. If you're used to highly fragranced shampoos you'll love these all-natural fragrances. They lather up a bit better and don't leave hair feeling as gritty as you rinse the product out.

Another option is to refill your shampoo and conditioner bottles from bulk at a health food store, or to purchase EWG-approved products.

Washing hair less frequently is another way to save on the amount of shampoo and plastic you might need, as well as to save water. Dermatologists tell us it's better for our hair and scalp health to wash less, anyway.

56. CREATE A BEAUTY ROUTINE THAT DOESN'T HARM THE EARTH: MAKEUP, APPLICATORS, AND REMOVERS.

It's important to me that my beauty routine doesn't impact others or the earth. By greening our makeup routines, we reduce plastic waste and the use of harmful chemicals.

INVESTMENT:
–

EFFORT:

TIME:

IMPACT:

The most eco option of all would be to skip makeup entirely, going for a more natural beauty look. There's no better way to teach our children (and friends' children) that people are beautiful as they are.

For makeup, check your favorites in the EWG database. Opt for brands with fewer ingredients, recyclable or compostable packaging, and the leaping bunny symbol that tells you they're cruelty-free.

For application, look for high-quality makeup brushes that will last for years. Bamboo, sustainably sourced wood, or recycled plastic can be a good choice for handles. Bristles are a bit more challenging; animal hair was the industry standard for decades, but big makeup companies are moving away from this for ethical and environmental reasons. I opt for cruelty-free and environmentally friendly brushes. For example, 100% Pure brand makes all their brushes from recycled water bottles. EcoTools makes brushes from recycled materials, with bamboo handles, and sells them in tree-free packaging made from bamboo and cotton fiber.

How about removal? The zero-waste store not far from me sells organic cotton and other colorful cotton makeup remover pads. These are far more sustainable than something that's continually being manufactured only to be thrown away, not to mention there's no plastic involved. If I didn't want to be so fancy, any rags from cut-up cotton clothing would work well. Just rinse out makeup and put into the washer after use.

My makeup remover is aloe and glycerin; you can buy these in bulk and experiment with making your own. I've also seen zero-waste makeup remover sold online.

57. LOOK FOR SUSTAINABLE TOWELS.

Cotton is marketed to us as natural and sustainable. It can be, but most is sprayed copiously with pesticides, and cotton cloth undergoes toxic bleaching and dyeing processes that create extensive amounts of wastewater. One T-shirt, for example, takes half a pound of pesticides to produce, so you can imagine a thick cotton towel might take more.

INVESTMENT:

EFFORT:

TIME:

IMPACT:

Organic cotton towels are available from many online retailers. Not ready to make that much of an investment? Sometimes retailers like Target sell towels that are "Standard 100 by OEKO-TEX certified." OEKO-TEX is a certification process that ensures the end product is free of 100 toxic chemicals ranging from pesticide residues to heavy metals and carcinogens that might have been used in dyes (OEKO-TEX 2020). There's no guarantee your OEKO-TEX-certified textiles were grown sustainably, but at least you know the end product is safe, which presumably equates to some safer manufacturing methods, too.

58. SHAVE AND WAX SUSTAINABLY.

Americans throw away about two billion razors annually (Environmental Protection Agency, 1990). Any step you take here can help reduce plastic waste.

INVESTMENT:
–

EFFORT:
◖ – ◖

TIME:
🕐

IMPACT:

Some folks prefer to stop shaving altogether, or to shave less often. This is certainly an easy solution, and we should be raising our kids to see either choice as valid.

Online zero-waste stores sell old-fashioned safety razors that are reusable. The replaceable metal blades can be recycled.

I use a razor with replaceable heads; however, in researching for this book I learned that by some estimates, if everyone in New York City used this sort of razor we'd end up with a collection of razor heads equal in weight to 324 elephants *every year.*

Electric razors provide a more sustainable option than disposable razors, even with their use of electricity, which is nominal. The issue is the waste generated in their production and disposal.

Waxing is another option that can be made sustainable. For example, MOOM sells an all-natural sugar wax with only three ingredients that comes in a glass jar with reusable and compostable cotton strips.

59. PROTECT YOURSELF AGAINST ANOTHER TP SHORTAGE.

The 2020 COVID-19 pandemic illustrated just how attached Americans are to their toilet paper. The issue with our beloved TP is that it destroys trees, takes a whole lot of water to make, uses toxic bleach, and then gets wrapped in petroleum-based plastics. For every roll of toilet paper you don't use, you save 37 gallons of water, 1.3 kilowatt hours of electricity, and about 1.5 pounds of wood (Earth Talk 2009). But there are easy alternatives.

INVESTMENT:

EFFORT:

TIME:

IMPACT:

You can buy TP made from recycled paper and non-chlorine bleach. (Bonus if it's wrapped in paper rather than plastic.)

Online retailers such as Who Gives a Crap sell toilet paper made out of bamboo. The plus side is that they only sell in bulk, so you'll be stocked up for the next pandemic.

If your budget allows and you own your home, install a bidet. The 2020 pandemic might prove to be just what Americans needed to get on board with the rest of the developed world's use of bidets. To save space and money, or if you rent your home, companies now sell small bidet devices that attach to your toilet seat, ranging from ones that heat the water and allow you to monitor water pressure to simple hoses, often used for rinsing cloth diapers.

Family cloth is another option. Taking its name from the cloth diapering movement, family cloth refers to using cloth rags to wipe. Some families use these in conjunction with a bidet, to dry off afterward. Other folks use them for urine only and save the TP for bowel movements. Some families are comfortable rinsing and then sanitizing rags for all their toilet duties.

60. CHOOSE MENSTRUAL CARE THAT CARES FOR THE EARTH, TOO.

There's a whole new world of sustainable menstrual products, and while it takes a bit of courage to switch from your comfortable routines, think how much more comfortable you'll be knowing you aren't putting bleach and plastics in or around your tender parts, not to mention keeping them out of the oceans and land.

INVESTMENT:

EFFORT:

TIME:

IMPACT:

Period panties are underwear with built-in pads that can be washed and re-worn. The top layer is wicking and they're generally much thinner than a pad, providing a high level of comfort to users. Do your research online; some brands have been found to contain toxic chemicals for absorption, whereas others test clean.

Menstrual cups are made with silicone or rubber (avoid plastic ones for obvious reasons) and are inserted into the vagina to catch menstrual flow. Users report a bit of a learning curve and suggest trying your cup first on at-home days, or with a backup pad.

Reusable pads are usually made from cotton or hemp.

Sea sponges are sustainably harvested, biodegradable, and reusable. They're inserted in the vagina to soak up blood.

Finally, if you want to stick with traditional pads or tampons, look for ones made with organic cotton, no bleach, and no plastics.

Chapter Five

Keeping House: Cleaning, Maintenance, and Life Admin

We all have our routines for maintaining our homes and vehicles, paying our bills, and so on. They present multiple opportunities for increasing sustainability, producing less waste while saving money, and simplifying our lives. This chapter presents options for dealing with your mail, batteries, home improvement, cleaning, energy use, furnishings, plant and lawn care, pest removal, and clothing.

61. JUNK THE JUNK MAIL.

Gone are the days when our mailboxes held a letter with a handwritten address bearing news from a distant friend or loved one. Today, every American receives the equivalent of 1.5 trees, worth of junk mail annually, and by some estimates will spend eight months of their life opening junk mail (West 2019). These easy options should greatly reduce the amount of mail you get overall, creating less deforestation and trash.

INVESTMENT:

EFFORT:

TIME:

IMPACT:

Opt out of offers that come in the mail from the prescreening of your credit score. Fill out a form online to opt out for five years, or print out and send in the form to opt out for good: OptOutPrescreen.com.

Fill out a form and pay $2 to be removed from Direct Mail Association marketing lists for a decade: dmachoice.thedma.org.

Sign up for online billing, payments, and banking.

Contact companies directly and ask them to remove you from mailing lists.

Recycle the junk mail you do receive.

62. BE CONSCIOUS ABOUT CLEAN CLOTHING.

Did you know most laundry products are a primary cause of indoor air pollution? That "clean" smell is a toxic chemical cocktail of potential carcinogens, reproductive toxins, and asthma and allergy triggers (Jaslow 2011; Science Daily 2008). Fabric softeners are especially bad because they coat our clothing with a progressive buildup of allergy-inducing fragrances, toxins, and potential carcinogens

(Sutton 2011). Greening your laundry puts less demand on production and disposal of toxic chemicals, reduces reliance on plastic containers, and requires less gas or electricity.

INVESTMENT: EFFORT:

TIME: IMPACT:

Look for eco-friendly detergents, or at least "free and clear" ones that don't have as much fragrance.

If you have access to a health food store, see about reusing your laundry containers to buy detergent from their bulk section.

Online zero-waste stores offer options such as laundry cubes or laundry strips that dissolve in water.

To soften clothes and reduce static cling, try adding vinegar to your washer's rinse cycle or using felted wool balls in your dryer.

Finally, don't forget to use a solar dryer, better known as a clothesline.

63. CLEAN CONSCIOUSLY.

Remember that cleaning supply chemicals are not closely regulated in the United States and contain many known toxins.

INVESTMENT: EFFORT:

TIME: IMPACT:

Simplify your cleaning routine. You don't really need one cleaner for the sink, another for counters, another for the stove, and so on. Most items can be cleaned with an all-purpose product. Check your EWG app for a safe one.

Make your own cleaners. Baking soda, lemon, vinegar, and essential oils are primary ingredients in healthy antibacterial or scouring cleaning products. You can verify the ingredients in your recipes via Google Scholar to see how effective they are. Remember, essential oils are natural (when purchased from a reputable company) but they're also highly concentrated plant chemicals that can cause harm, especially to pets, infants, children, and people with breathing issues.

Look for reusable mops rather than ones with disposable cloths.

Skip the scrubby kitchen sponges that are made from polyester or nylon that turns into pervasive microplastics. Purchase plastic-free brushes made of sustainably sourced wood or bamboo and natural fiber bristles. Use a little baking soda to scour, or reuse onion bags (remember to purchase onions loose next time, if possible) wrapped around a sponge or rag for extra scrubbing power. Sustainable kitchen scrubbies reduce our reliance on plastic and cut waste because they're biodegradable.

Make your own reusable rags from old clothing. Flannel can be cut or sewn into wonderful replacements for paper towels. Check out Swedish dishcloths, which can be washed up to 200 times, soak up far more than a paper towel, and are fully biodegradable. Bonus? They come in all sorts of fun prints.

64. DON'T WASTE YOUR ENERGY.

We're all about reducing our energy bill, but the biggest savings come in reducing climate-impacting emissions generated by power production. Right now, energy-related emissions are predicted to increase 70 percent by 2050 (Thompson 2014).

INVESTMENT:	EFFORT:
	◗-◖
TIME:	IMPACT:
◷	

Many electric companies now give you the option to pay a few dollars extra for solar or wind power. I've even gotten offers in the mail to switch to sustainably sourced power with a guaranteed reduction in my energy use bill. Check with your energy company to see what options are available to you.

Turn off lights and other items when not in use. Electronics continue to draw low levels of power when off, so plug home electronics into a power strip and turn off the power at the strip. Bonus? Using power strips is not only safer for electronics and your electrical system, but you can also reduce your electric bill by about 5 percent.

Purchase a $20 Kill A Watt electricity monitor. Plug it in behind your refrigerator or other major appliances to test their efficiency.

Keep your refrigerator running efficiently by keeping coils clean, letting food cool a bit before putting it inside, and not letting its internal temperature run too cold.

Your clothes dryer is another major user of electricity or gas. Hang clothing to dry whenever possible. A small drying rack in a laundry room or bedroom can save you a good deal of money and add humidity to dry winter air.

65. TURN YOUR TRASH INTO SOMEONE ELSE'S TREASURE.

You know the saying: "One person's trash is another person's treasure." Selling and donating allows items to be reused rather than ending up in a landfill, thereby reducing consumption of goods.

INVESTMENT:	EFFORT:
	◗
TIME:	**IMPACT:**
◷	

Identify your nearest thrift store, clean out, and donate. It feels so good to clear out space, and you are not adding to landfill waste.

Sell unused items online or have a garage sale.

Put a notice on social media: "X item. Free for Pickup." Facebook Marketplace, eBay, Craigslist, Freecycle, and the Buy Nothing Project are all great resources for letting your old items find a new life.

66. EMBRACE THE HOUSEPLANT.

Green plants in your house do a lot besides make it friendly and beautiful.

INVESTMENT:

EFFORT:

TIME:

IMPACT:

Houseplants can help rid our homes of air pollution. Studies have found that plants can absorb VOCs, one of the harmful waste products that off-gasses from a wide variety of household items (Kobayashi, et al. 2007).

Scientific studies also show that they're good for boosting our mood, enhancing our immune systems, relaxing us, helping us concentrate, and even keeping a humidity level in our home that reduces transmission of flu viruses (Bringslimark, et al. 2008; Burchett 2010; Fjeld 1998, 2002).

If you have a cat, be cautious. Many plants are poisonous to cats who may curiously take a nibble. Look online for the best plants for air quality or cat safety.

67. EMBRACE FREE AND LOW-COST WAYS TO REDUCE INDOOR AIR POLLUTION.

These methods help reduce the amount of chemicals used in production and protect the air quality in your home so you're not breathing in toxic air waste.

INVESTMENT: EFFORT:

TIME: IMPACT:

Remove your shoes at the door. Studies have found that our shoes contain pesticide residues, toxins from roads, and harmful bacteria such as E. coli, staph, and C. diff from places like public bathrooms (Bryce 2019). Who wants that in their homes? You especially want to avoid tracking in unhealthy materials if you have pets and small children.

Open your windows on nice, clear days. Airing out the house for a few minutes, even on a cold but fresh winter day, is a good way to flush out winter germs.

Freshen up your home with non-toxic fragrances from herbs and essential oils. Place fresh lavender, rose petals, or other aromatic herbs in an old scrap of fabric and tie it into a bundle. You can also sew a small pillow-type sachet to keep dresser drawers, linen storage, and kitchen cabinets fresh. Some herbs can help repel pests.

High-quality essential oils can provide fragrance in homemade cleaning products or via a diffuser. Choose oils for their antibacterial or antiviral properties, or to enhance mood, whether uplifting or relaxing. Dilute properly and diffuse for no more than 30 to 60 minutes at a time. Remember to check which oils are safe for children and pets (Hogan 2019; New Directions Aromatics 2019).

Cedar blocks can be hung in closets to keep items fresh and to repel moths and mice.

Look for candles scented with essential oils only, made with lead-free wicks, and composed of sustainably sourced oils. Most candles are made from paraffin wax that off-gasses up to 22 toxic chemicals into your home (Environment, Health and Safety Online 2020). At first, these might smell a bit odd and earthy to you, but you'll quickly adjust and start to notice the unhealthy, sickly-sweet chemical smell in artificial fragrances.

68. RECHARGE—ALL ABOUT BATTERIES.

Batteries are a commonplace household item that easily fall under the "reduce, reuse, and recycle" axiom. Batteries contain known carcinogens and dangerous metals that leach into our land and water (Call2Recycle 2020). Reducing, reusing, and recycling them protects our water and health.

INVESTMENT:

EFFORT:

TIME:

IMPACT:

Reduce your need for batteries by avoiding battery-operated toys and gadgets when possible.

Invest in a battery charger and purchase reusable batteries for those you do need. Shop for batteries with the highest number of cycles.

Call2Recycle.org provides options for dropping off batteries locally or shipping them to recycling centers.

69. HEAD DOWN THE ROAD TOWARD AN (ALMOST) ZERO-WASTE AUTOMOBILE.

Whether you are in the market for a new car or taking care of the car you have, here are some ways to get closer to zero waste.

INVESTMENT:

EFFORT:

TIME:

IMPACT:

Tune-ups, oil changes, and changing your vehicle's air filter as needed will reduce emissions and gasoline use, make your vehicle safer and longer-lasting, and protect the air inside the vehicle itself.

Speaking of the air in your automobile, skip the little air fresheners. They pollute your air with toxic off-gassing, increase demand for the chemicals that produce them, and result in plastic wrappers and waste in landfills (Gregorio 2018; Environmental Working Group 2020). Instead, dab a wooden clothespin with essential oils and clip it to your air vents or place an herbal sachet on your dash.

New vehicles off-gas hundreds of chemicals (Warner 2012). For this reason, I only buy used. If your vehicle still has that new car smell, open the windows to air it out, especially on warm days.

My vehicle has a gas mileage gauge that helps me drive more efficiently and save gasoline. Coasting down hills, using less pressure on the gas pedal, coasting to stops, and using cruise control on highways are all ways to improve your mileage and help reduce our reliance on petroleum. If it's an electric or biodiesel vehicle, all the better.

Don't forget that making fewer trips, carpooling via ride share services, taking public transportation, and good old-fashioned walking and bike riding are even better.

70. REDUCE VOCS IN HOME IMPROVEMENT.

Many of our home improvement items are full of toxic chemicals (Environmental Working Group 2019). Fortunately, green building supplies are on the increase. Green building helps reduce chemical production, as well as air pollution inside and outside.

INVESTMENT:
–

EFFORT:
◖-◖

TIME:
🕐

IMPACT:

When you paint your home, look for low- or zero-VOC paints. Want to be extra careful? Order beautiful, healthy paints from BioShield. They also make wood stains for inside and outside use and natural hardwood floor finishes.

Need plumbing goop or other adhesive? Look for ones with low odor.

Shop for wood that's certified sustainable and consider more environmentally friendly insulation like wool, cotton, or recycled cellulose. If spray foam is your choice, look for ones made from vegetable oils rather than petroleum.

Need to remodel a bathroom or kitchen? Look for cabinets that use sustainable materials and have low to no off-gassing of formaldehyde, a toxic component of particleboard. Check out places like Habitat for Humanity ReStore or retailers like IKEA that go above and beyond to adhere to stringent environmental regulations.

71. REMEMBER: PLASTIC IS NOT SO FANTASTIC.

Plastic kid toys, pet toys, dishes, storage containers, hangers, refrigerators, beds, and furniture—and I'm typing this sentence on a plastic keyboard. It's difficult to get away from our reliance on petroleum, which is why every step we can take is so very important. We add our drops in the bucket to shift our culture away from petroleum reliance and reduce the amount of microplastics that end up in our earth and water.

INVESTMENT:	EFFORT:
–	◗
TIME:	IMPACT:
🕐	▨ ▨ ▨

When you buy *any* new item, look for one that isn't plastic. If you're working to reduce consumption all around, you'll have a bit extra to pay for some non-plastic items.

72. USE SAFER METHODS OF PEST REMOVAL.

Nobody wants mice or roaches in the house or fleas and ticks in the yard. Most pesticides remain in the environment, creating toxic waste

in our air and water that harms humans and animals and kills beneficial insects that pollinate our food crops (Kovach 1992).

INVESTMENT:

−

TIME:

EFFORT:

IMPACT:

If you live in a colder climate, don't spray unless there's a problem. If you're in a warmer area where spraying is routine, look
for safer options like an all-natural, essential oil–based pesticide
found at Lowe's.

I get ants in my house annually, and sometimes fruit flies. For
these, I get Terro brand's borax-based traps for ants and fruit flies.
While borax is a natural substance, it's still very harmful to small
creatures, so keep it away from pets.

For major pest issues, seek companies that do eco-friendly or organic
pest removal. Don't believe the marketing that all pesticides are
friendly. Go to Google Scholar and research the chemicals yourself.

In the yard, beneficial nematodes and guinea hens can help with fleas
and/or ticks. Most flea and tick medications cause harmful side effects
and creates waste in manufacturing and disposal. Talk to a holistic vet
about safer alternatives.

73. DRESS FOR (EARTH'S) SUCCESS.

You'll recall that textile waste makes up a huge portion of what's
dumped in our landfills annually. Gone are the days when people purchased clothing made to last. Today, we have "fast fashion," an entire
industry of inexpensive, trendy, disposable clothing that seldom lasts
more than a season. The impact of this industry on air and water pollution is astronomical, not to mention the child and sweatshop labor it

often involves. Check out the documentary *The True Cost* if you want to learn more (Morgan 2015).

INVESTMENT:

EFFORT:

TIME:

IMPACT:

The first step is always to reduce. Learn about creating a capsule wardrobe with a handful of items that can be used to create multiple outfits. Instead of investing in every new trend seasonally, find simple ways to update your capsule wardrobe to stay on trend. In the long run, you'll save a good deal of money and reduce waste.

Reuse; thrift stores are often great sources for vintage items, business casual wear, evening wear, and jeans and sweaters. Host a clothing swap with a group of friends.

Recycle—or in this case, upcycle. If you're handy with a sewing machine, there's a whole world of gorgeous upcycled clothing inspiration online. I've seen denim with embroidery, men's shirts turned into dresses, and wool items felted and sewn into myriad other items. Create your own haute couture. Decorative mending can transform an old piece of clothing into a work of art.

When you purchase new, use all the money you've saved to go organic. I'm a big fan of Pact Organic, especially when they have sales, for leggings, undergarments, dresses, and hoodies. My other go-tos are Blue Canoe (though I typically only shop their final sales), along with Athleta, which uses some organic and recycled fabrics.

Clothing is like art for the body, a means of self-expression. Look for sustainable high fashion, and check your current wardrobe for trends. For example, summer 2020 was all about both neutrals (you probably already have some) and neons. Opt for a neon silk scarf rather than a head-to-toe new outfit.

74. STABILIZE YOUR HOME CLIMATE WITHOUT IMPACTING THE EARTH'S CLIMATE.

The more you can do to reduce your need for heat and AC, the fewer natural resources you'll waste.

INVESTMENT:
–

EFFORT:
◐-○

TIME:
○-○○○

IMPACT:

Passive solar heating is the single best way to maintain temperature in a home. This building method places buildings and windows in such a way that they collect warmth from the sun, store it in the thermal mass of thick building materials such as concrete, and distribute warmth via radiation and convection systems. In warm weather, these buildings are designed to shade the sun. Such homes are not excessively expensive to build, and return on investment is immediate.

Most of us are probably not building a new home, though. Want to know where your home is leaking heat and cooled air? A free energy audit from your utility company will let you know exactly where to seal things up.

County programs frequently offer free energy upgrades such as thermal-paned windows and insulation. These greatly reduce dependency on heating systems which, in turn, cut heating and cooling costs.

Heating a home with electricity can potentially be more eco-friendly than heating with propane or natural gas; however, electric heat can get expensive. Wood furnaces and wood stoves can be another green option, depending on the source of the wood.

75. LOOK FOR THE ENERGY STAR RATING.

Energy Star appliances typically use 30 percent less energy on average than other appliances, helping sustain the environment and protect your wallet from high utility bills.

INVESTMENT:

EFFORT:

TIME:

IMPACT:

If you need a new appliance, you might look for a used one first. Most new appliances, even many used ones, can now be purchased with an Energy Star certification. Look for that symbol on dishwashers, refrigerators, washers and dryers, and small kitchen appliances, too. (You can even get an Energy Star–rated front door.)

Beyond Energy Star ratings, there are things you can do for little or no money to maximize the efficiency of your home electronics and appliances. Google "how to make my fridge more efficient" or "maximize my heating efficiency."

76. GET DOWN WITH SUSTAINABLE FLOORING.

Like mattresses and furniture, our petroleum-derived rugs can be toxic. Even synthetic rugs often have a peculiar smell due to the off-gassing of harmful VOCs. Remember: toxic off-gassing is waste, and we are trying to eliminate it.

INVESTMENT:

EFFORT:

TIME:

IMPACT:

Many of our flooring materials are plastic-based, so when possible, opt for real wood that's been sustainably sourced, with a non-toxic sealer.

Real linoleum is made from wood fibers, not plastic. Ceramic tile is also a better option. While not fully biodegradable, it does break down to a non-toxic dust.

For wall-to-wall carpet, look for organic wool or cotton. For bare floors, look for wool, cotton, jute, sisal, or other natural-fiber area rugs. They produce less waste in production and less pollution to water and air, and can compost rather than create microplastic waste. I purchase wool or cotton area rugs at big-box discount stores.

Moving into a new apartment? Ask if it's standard for the apartment to install new carpet for each tenant. If it is, maybe you can negotiate a discount by opting out of new carpet, with which you could purchase a non-toxic carpet cleaner and rent a steamer.

77. GREEN UP YOUR LAWN.

Have a lawn? You've probably seen the humorous meme about how we've been duped into mowing our lawns under the belief that this is a normal and necessary part of life. Aside from the time spent, most mowers rely on petroleum products.

INVESTMENT:
–

EFFORT:

TIME:

IMPACT:

You might want to take the no-lawn idea seriously. Convert a large portion or all of your lawn to gardens. You'll reduce waste by needing less gas or electricity to mow, not to mention the joys of growing your own food and flowers and watching bees and butterflies thrive.

Have a large lawn? Convert a portion of it to a meadow by not mowing; more greenery means more clean air.

Putting in a new lawn? Instead of grass, plant a low-growing native species such as clover. Contact your local Cooperative Extension office to learn what plants are native to your area. Not only will there be no need to mow, you'll also find that native species don't demand as much water in some geographic regions, so you'll be further reducing your use of natural resources.

Battery-operated lawnmowers, while a slightly higher upfront investment, avoid the need for gas and oil and don't pollute the air.

Finally, ignore the myth that your lawn must be sprayed and fertilized regularly, and befriend the dandelions, plantains, and other green weeds. You'll save money while protecting the air and water, children and animals, and yourself from the waste created by chemical production and spraying. Dandelions and plantains are powerfully medicinal, too.

78. GET A HEALTHY NIGHT'S SLEEP.

Imagine spending one-third of your life sleeping on a bed of petro-chemicals blanketed with allergy and asthma triggers, plus a few carcinogens thrown in for fun. This is what most of us do on a daily basis. Not only do these harm us, they also deplete fossil fuels and create extensive water and air waste during manufacturing. In tests, mattresses have been found to off-gas up to 61 toxic chemicals (Environmental Working Group 2019; Sleep Advisor 2020). By purchasing a more sustainable mattress that can decompose after use, you also reduce the 15 to 20 million mattresses taking up 132 thousand square miles of US landfills annually (Blanchard 2018).

INVESTMENT:

EFFORT:
◐ - ◐

TIME:
🕐

IMPACT:

Can't afford a new mattress? Order an organic cotton, wool, or latex rubber mattress topper. When possible, sleep with your window cracked open an inch or more for fresh air. I keep mine open in all but the most frigid winter weather.

Purchase healthier organic mattresses for infants and children, whose bodies are still developing.

When you're ready to invest in a new one, check out My Green Mattress, my No. 1 pick for price and quality. Their mattresses are made of real latex rubber and organic cotton and/or wool. Latex has antimicrobial properties that can reduce the risks of mold, dust mites, and other allergens in your mattress. Plus, it's biodegradable. Wool provides a safe alternative to chemical fire retardants that are required by law to be in mattresses.

When purchasing a mattress, look for things like organic cotton and wool, 100 percent rubber latex, Global Organic Textile Standard (GOTS) certification, low VOC-certified (for non-natural foams), Greenguard Gold, or OEKO-TEX 100 certification.

Buying an all-natural or organic mattress reduces plastic and chemical waste in production and disposal and shrinks the toxic chemical air pollution in your home. If you live in California, Connecticut, or Rhode Island, you can recycle your old mattress, no matter what kind it is.

79. LOUNGE SUSTAINABLY.

Furniture has many of the same issues as mattresses. Most of it is made from petroleum-derived foams, often using unsustainably sourced wood or particleboard that off-gasses. Whatever step you take, you'll be closer to reducing toxic waste in our air and water and landfills.

INVESTMENT:

EFFORT:
◖-◯

TIME:
◷-◷◷

IMPACT:

Simple wood chairs and benches, or sitting on the floor, are healthier for our bodies. I admire folks who are willing to give up their furniture, but I'm not ready to take that step.

Buy used when possible.

Companies like Pottery Barn, West Elm, and IKEA offer somewhat more sustainable options. IKEA adheres to tighter European manufacturing standards and applies the strictest global standards to their products. They work to eliminate toxic chemicals, and often use innovative methods to reduce emissions to levels far lower than legal limits require.

Look for furniture that is made from sustainably sourced woods and recycled components, has low formaldehyde off-gassing, and uses CertiPUR-certified foams that are made with fewer toxins. The same certifications and standards mentioned above also apply to mattresses.

Try making your own furniture if you have the space and tools. Start with simple garden furniture designs. Purchase organic cotton fabric and experiment with stuffing it with wool or cotton, or a carefully cut-up, real latex mattress topper.

If you are ready to spring for an all-organic sofa, The Futon Shop and other online retailers offer multiple organic sofa styles with free shipping. Some let you customize your filling and/or fabrics. Prices begin around $2,000.

80. HARNESS THE POWER OF THE SUN.

Energy from the sun can help us reduce our reliance on fossil fuels, and it's readily available.

INVESTMENT:

EFFORT:

TIME:

IMPACT:

Installing solar panels on your property is a great way to reduce your reliance on the grid and generate free, sustainable power. Some areas even allow you to sell excess electricity back to the grid or offer tax breaks for solar installation.

If you're handy, you might be able to install your own. There are all sorts of DIY options. Various programs allow you to purchase or lease solar panels. The time it takes to recoup your initial monetary investment will vary, but you'll know from day one that you're doing something to save the environment.

Can't swing solar panels? Consider installing a solar hot water heater or solar-powered outdoor lights.

Chapter Six

Daily Life: Work and School

Your zero-waste efforts don't have to be confined to your homelife. You can lessen the environmental footprint of your work and school life with the steps in this chapter.

Some of these steps are simple enough to take at home with a little bit of forethought and preparation, and others will need cooperation from your colleagues or schoolmates. The latter, in particular, have the potential to create quite large impacts. Remember to respect others where they are; think back to when zero waste was a daunting journey you weren't yet ready to embark on. Start small and build on the positive feelings of success.

81. BEGIN YOUR DAY WITH BREAKFAST AT HOME.

The overwhelming rush out the door in the morning prompts us to grab something fast and easy, often with no regard to health or waste. A quick, healthy breakfast from home can reduce takeout waste, save money, and potentially be healthier.

INVESTMENT:

EFFORT:

TIME:

IMPACT:

If you need to eat on the go, plan ahead. Overnight oats or chia seed pudding in a canning jar are fast to make and perfect for grab and go. You can find plenty of easy recipes online. Baked breakfast bars or muffins require a bit more planning, but offer all-week breakfasts in return.

Smoothies or homemade breakfast burritos with tofu or eggs and a bit of last night's leftover veggies require minimal morning prep and can easily be taken to go. My favorite fast breakfast is a green smoothie with spinach, banana, berries, and water. A quick Internet search will provide oodles of smoothie inspiration.

To eliminate waste, use canning jars, silicone bags, compostable wax bags, beeswax wraps, and reusable coffee mugs.

When you do stop at your favorite coffee shop, bring your own mug and ask them to hand you the muffin or pastry without a bag. You can immediately wrap it in your own cloth napkin or small reusable bag.

82. REDUCE YOUR COMMUTE.

There is little positive to be said about the 2020 COVID-19 pandemic, but one good thing is that cities saw a dramatic reduction in smog because far fewer automobiles were on the road. Hopefully, we can work toward a new "normal" that embraces practices that create blue skies and help reduce our reliance on petroleum.

INVESTMENT:

EFFORT:

TIME:

IMPACT:

Walk or bike to work if possible. Imagine how good you'd feel if your daily workout got you to work and reduced emissions in the process.

Public transportation is another great option, greatly reducing the number of vehicles on the road. There's nothing like sitting comfortably on a train while whizzing by a traffic jam.

Consider carpooling. Park-and-ride spots provide good access points to public transportation and a great place to meet a coworker and carpool. Do an Internet search for rideshare apps to connect you with the right commuters.

Encourage your school, university, or workplace to create policies that favor non-vehicular commutes, such as well-lit bus stops and safe places to lock up bikes.

See if you can eliminate your commute entirely at least a few days per week. COVID-19 taught us that working from home is a more viable option than some companies realized.

83. GO PAPER-FREE.

According to Record Nations, employees spend up to 30 to 40 percent of each day looking for records kept in file cabinets, and an estimated 70 percent of businesses would fail if they lost records in floods or fire. Today there's little genuine need for paper, yet we use 65,390,000,000 sheets of paper daily in the United States alone, and this number is growing annually (O'Mara 2020). Whatever steps you take to cut back on paper, you'll be saving trees that clean our

environment and reducing the water waste and air and water pollution from paper manufacturing.

INVESTMENT:

EFFORT:

TIME:

IMPACT:

Consider tech alternatives. GoodNotes works like a digital notebook.
Smartphone calendars take the place of paper planners, and cloud
storage allows easy sharing of documents. Apps and software for
digital signatures abound. If you feel more productive with a piece of
paper in hand, purchase recycled or tree-free paper, use scrap paper,
and be sure to recycle.

Set up an appointment at your child's school and with their teachers
about going paper-free. Most kids come home with multiple papers
in their backpacks each week. These can get lost, crumpled, and dirty.
A simple email and online signature could streamline the process,
making everyone's lives easier. Teachers would save time, kids
wouldn't have to manage papers, and parents wouldn't need to hunt
for them, sign them, and make sure they end up in the backpack.

Urge your child's school to create a system where parents can opt in
for emails and digital signatures at the beginning of the year. Keep the
paper option for folks who don't have tech at home.

Think about how many things at work could be passed around
digitally rather than in print. Consider having people pull out their
smartphones to view a document during meetings, rather than
using handouts.

84. REUSE PAPER AND OPT FOR SUSTAINABLE PAPERS.

When I was in college, I lived 10 miles from a paper factory. The stench
from it was unbelievable at times. Not only does reducing and reusing

paper save trees, which clean our air, it also reduces the amount of air and water pollution that stem from paper manufacturing.

INVESTMENT:

EFFORT:

TIME:

IMPACT:

Sometimes paper is necessary. Be sure to print on both sides of the paper and use both sides of note or sketch pads when possible. Failed print jobs make great paper for quick handwritten notes, or to print an office-wide note to hang on a bulletin board.

A largely paperless office will save a tremendous amount of money, some of which can be used to purchase tree-free, bleach-free, or recycled paper for the things that do need to be printed.

85. GO DIGITAL FOR TEXTBOOKS, EXAMS, AND HOMEWORK.

Between textbooks, homework, and papers, education is responsible for a tremendous amount of paper waste. Many of today's freshman classes at state universities have more than 300 students per class. Imagine the paper saved if all their research papers and tests were turned in digitally. Imagine the collective impact if this became standard practice around the nation.

INVESTMENT:

EFFORT:

TIME:

IMPACT:

If you've purchased textbooks, you've probably gasped at the cost. Renting is a less expensive option, but digital textbooks still come out on top as the least expensive and most eco-friendly option.

If you're an instructor, encourage your students to use e-books. Provide them with tests they can take online, and encourage homework to be turned in via email. Not only will you reduce paper consumption and waste, you'll also find grading goes faster when you're not trying to decipher handwriting.

Use the money saved through reduced use of paper to purchase sustainable paper for the things that must be printed.

86. REDUCE POWER CONSUMPTION AT WORK AND SCHOOL.

How many office buildings have you entered on a hot summer day only to find them freezing cold? The larger your organization, the larger the impact will be.

INVESTMENT:	EFFORT:

TIME:	IMPACT:

Your company can save money with small temperature changes while reducing the draw on unsustainable power sources.

Encourage others to use computers that drain less power. For example, set screens to go idle when not in use. Unplug external equipment like webcams or printers, and keep screen brightness only as high as necessary. Unplug laptops when they are fully charged.

Use smart power strips for office equipment. These reduce "vampire loads," the subtle but constant draw on electricity when a device is plugged in but turned off. Smart power strips detect when a device is turned off and stop the flow of electricity. For these devices to work, computers, printers, copy machines, and so on need to be turned off at the end of the day.

87. BRING YOUR OWN LUNCH.

Packing your own lunch is one of the best ways to reduce waste and save money.

INVESTMENT:	EFFORT:
	◑

TIME:	IMPACT:
🕐	

If ordering in or eating out is the norm at your workplace, suggest a weekly lunch potluck with coworkers.

When you do eat out, choose restaurants that allow you to dine in, using reusable rather than disposable dinnerware, or identify takeout locations that favor reduced or zero waste. And use your own napkins, silverware, and cups with takeout.

88. THINK SUSTAINABLE WHEN IT COMES TO OFFICE AND SCHOOL GIFTS.

Secret Santas, school valentines, your boss's birthday, and white elephant gifts all have a tendency to generate waste.

INVESTMENT:	EFFORT:
	◑

TIME:	IMPACT:
🕐	

Consider sustainable gifts like locally made specialty foods, homemade goodies, movie tickets, and lottery tickets. These are fun ideas with little to no waste involved. For a white elephant, consider throwing in a package of Who Gives a Crap's brightly wrapped tree-free toilet paper for that added touch of humor. If you Google "sustainable white elephant gifts," you'll come up with loads of other fun gift ideas as well.

Don't be a party pooper when you see the waste created. It might hurt your heart, but our examples can be more impactful than our words. A gracious and humble attitude will get you further than loud protests and bitter, critical comments. Live your values with grace.

Your earth-friendly ways are likely to be noticed by coworkers who are interested in reducing waste, too.

89. USE SMARTPHONE CAMERAS FOR COPIES.

Why copy things when you can simply take a picture? We have the ultimate "photo" copier right in our hands.

INVESTMENT:

EFFORT:

TIME:

IMPACT:

A friend of mine directs a program for teens; instead of printing multiple papers for handouts, she prints just one, and the kids take a picture of it. This strategy not only cuts paper use, it also makes it easier for the kids to keep track of the handouts and refer back to them later.

90. GO ZERO-WASTE IN YOUR DORM ROOM.

Going off to college is often the first step in creating an independent life. There's no better time to also begin your (almost) zero-waste journey. Here are 10 ideas to get you started.

INVESTMENT:

EFFORT:

TIME:

IMPACT:

Look through chapter 4 and choose toiletries and towels that are (almost) zero-waste.

Buy sustainable school supplies.

Choose non-plastics, as much as possible, for storage, hangers, dishes, and so on.

Invest in a small crockpot and cookbook that allow you to more easily make zero-waste meals from bulk food items.

Make a list of takeout places that let you bring your own containers or offer recyclable containers.

Look for cozy bedding made from natural fibers rather than poly.

Invest in an essential oil diffuser and a few high-quality organic oils or an all-natural essential oil–based air freshener.

Decorate with art and décor made by yourself or your friends, or bought on Etsy. Avoid plastics as much as possible.

Keep a small recycling bin in your room to make it easy for you and your roommates to recycle.

Invest in a small water filter and reusable (non-plastic) water bottle instead of purchasing plastic water bottles.

91. SET UP A REUSE NETWORK AT SCHOOL.

The more ways we have to reduce and reuse items, the less waste we'll generate. Setting up a used-items network with people you see daily is a great way to embody the value of "reusing"—diminishing consumption of goods and the waste that goes into their manufacture.

INVESTMENT:

EFFORT:
◐

TIME:
◐-◐ ◐

IMPACT:

Share your needs and pass along unused items. Use a bulletin board, email list, or social media page devoted to your school or organization to list free items or gently used items for sale.

Imagine if your university had a free textbook exchange. Bring a textbook, take a textbook. Or imagine if you could pass along school uniform items, or sell a barely used kitchen item to a coworker. If you can imagine it, you can create it.

92. PRESENT DAILY ZERO-WASTE IDEAS TO YOUR HUMAN RESOURCES (HR) DEPARTMENT.

A good HR department exists to create a healthy work environment for everyone. It should be open to new ideas; however, don't expect it to adopt your waste-cutting solutions without some effort on your part.

INVESTMENT:

EFFORT:

TIME:

IMPACT:

Provide HR with a brief presentation based on facts from reliable sources. Explain the issues succinctly and present easy-to-implement solutions for a zero-waste workplace—solutions based on where waste is created. Propose a timeline that calls for adoption of one change at a time. The key to making changes sustainable is to start with those that are most easily achievable, thereby creating a feeling of success and empowering people to want to take another step. (See chapter 10 for a template for proposing changes in a business or school.)

Perhaps the first step would be to put out a bin for recycling and to provide emails and reminders in meetings to please recycle. Keep track of how much is being recycled, then build on the positive: Thank everyone for their efforts and let them know the impact of these efforts. The second step could be getting everyone on board with online document sharing rather than handouts during meetings. Record Nations tells us that 45 percent of paper handouts in offices are trashed by the end of the day (O'Mara 2020).

Go slowly. Expect "mistakes" and focus on the positives. As you implement small changes, keep people posted on their success. Consider creating or looking for zero-waste informational flyers to hang in your break room that keep people focused on both the need for zero waste and the collective power of their positive choices.

See chapter 10 for more specifics on presenting ideas in the workplace or school.

93. COMPOST AT WORK AND SCHOOL.

According to FarmToSchool.org, public schools throw away 36.5 pounds of food per student annually, making up almost 2 percent of our annual food waste. Remember: Food waste in landfills can't decompose without oxygen, creating massive amounts of harmful methane emissions. Although food waste represents a small percentage of our waste, it's an easy one to reduce. Teaching kids about food waste helps them develop healthy habits, which they can bring home.

INVESTMENT:

EFFORT:

TIME:

IMPACT:

Friends of mine have teens who petitioned their school to compost. If you have school-to-cafeteria gardens (more on that in chapter 10), the compost can be used there. Otherwise, you can arrange for pickup from a local farm or compost service. Workplace compost systems can operate similarly.

Some schools and university cafeterias have created food-share tables with free items, and have found ways to turn leftovers into meals for homeless people.

Bring your own scraps home to compost rather than throwing them in the trash. Just pack them into your reusable lunch container or a jar carried for this purpose.

94. PROPOSE ECOLOGICAL VOLUNTEER DAYS AND ECO FIELD TRIPS.

Volunteer days and field trips provide an opportunity to step outside of normal work and school routines and to engage with the wider world.

INVESTMENT:

EFFORT:

TIME:

IMPACT:

Find out ahead of time when your workplace or school will be holding field trips or volunteer days. Research sustainable or environmental organizations in your area and see what opportunities they offer for group visits.

If you're a student, perhaps you'd like to do a science fair presentation on the work of one of these organizations and present sustainable, zero-waste ideas to your peers. Or you can arrange for someone to speak at your school or workplace on a relevant topic of sustainability.

By using field trips and volunteer days to engage in earth-friendly activities, you help nurture a love of nature in others. A positive experience helps people feel empowered to make a difference, and one positive experience can lead to another.

95. OFFSET YOUR BUSINESS'S CARBON FOOTPRINT.

A carbon footprint is the measurement of how much carbon and other climate-change emissions an individual, business, or trip creates (Carbon Footprint n.d.).

INVESTMENT:
–

EFFORT:

TIME:

IMPACT:

Use an online business carbon footprint calculator to estimate the amount of emissions your business generates annually. These calculators link to organizations you can donate to in ways that will offset your carbon footprint by planting trees, installing solar energy, or other sustainable measures.

Work with HR to create a fundraiser or other event that will help offset your business's carbon footprint.

96. SHOW YOUR CORPORATE AND SCHOOL SPIRIT WITHOUT THE INDIVIDUALLY WRAPPED FREEBIES.

Just because it's free doesn't mean you need it. Workplaces and schools generate a good deal of waste from individually wrapped promotional items printed with company or school logos.

INVESTMENT:
–

EFFORT:

TIME:

IMPACT:

If you're tempted to purchase, consider carefully and show your spirit with reusable items like a shirt instead of sticky notes or plastic pens. Ask your school bookstore to sell specific sustainable items that you'd prefer.

If you're in the marketing department, consider items that are not wrapped in plastic or headed for a landfill. Google "sustainable promotional products" or "eco-friendly promotional products" for ideas. You'll find things like reusable organic cotton bags, reusable straws and mugs, and backpacks made from recycled materials, all ready for your company's logo.

97. INVEST IN REUSABLES FOR THE BREAK ROOM.

Each of the small steps listed below adds up to major reductions in waste in a large workplace. When you consider thousands of other workplaces moving in the same direction, the reduction of waste will be huge.

INVESTMENT:

EFFORT:

TIME:

IMPACT:

Ask HR for reusables for the break room. See if coworkers have unused silverware, plates, mugs, and cups they want to donate. If not, pick up these reusable items at your local thrift store.

Encourage your company to skip the convenient single-pod coffee makers in favor of zero-waste or low-waste coffee options such as a French press or drip machine.

Look for changes specific to your own workplace. For example, if microwave popcorn is a popular snack, suggest pooling resources with coworkers to purchase a silicone microwave popcorn popper and a bulk glass jar of popcorn.

Encourage your workplace to install a water dispenser rather than selling single-use water bottles.

See chapter 10 for a full discussion on proposing changes in workplaces and schools.

98. SELL BULK SNACKS RATHER THAN INDIVIDUALLY WRAPPED VENDING MACHINE SNACKS.

Say goodbye to individually packaged snacks and hello to fulfillment of mid-afternoon snack attack cravings that are healthier for you and the earth.

INVESTMENT:
–

EFFORT:

TIME:

IMPACT:

If stores can offer things in bulk, why can't break rooms? You'll need permission from HR and a bit of organizational work, but this shouldn't be a very difficult change to make.

Popcorn, trail mix, dried mangos, fig cookies, crackers, and more are available in bulk bins at major grocery stores and health food stores. Provide a shelf full of large jars or containers of snacks. Attach a small measuring cup or scoop to each one, just as stores have. Set a price of so many dollars per scoop and put a change box nearby. (There will be bonus savings when employees use their own reusable containers.) Fresh fruit is another great option to offer for sale.

99. ENCOURAGE YOUR WORKPLACE TO BUY SUSTAINABLE ITEMS.

On a daily basis, our places of employment and education use toilet paper, paper towels, sanitizers, creamer and sugar for coffee, paper, ink, and much more. With a little thought and planning, you can cut down on waste and add your company's drop to the bucket.

INVESTMENT:
–

EFFORT:

TIME:

IMPACT:

Using recycled or tree-free toilet paper and paper towels eases the depletion of our forests, which in turn keeps our air and water cleaner.

Switching cleaning products to green ones with no fragrance reduces air and water waste in manufacturing and in the use of these items.

Buying organic cream and sugar in large containers rather than small individual packets reduces waste in both production and disposal.

Tree-free or recycled paper and refillable or recyclable ink cartridges also reduce waste.

100. CHOOSE (ALMOST) ZERO WASTE FOR OFFICE EVENTS.

Once you've gotten your workplace on board with the idea of zero waste in general, look for ways to make office events more sustainable, whether in food production, packaging waste, or food waste itself.

INVESTMENT:

EFFORT:

TIME:

IMPACT:

Bottles of water and prepackaged snacks are often available at meetings. Would your coworkers consider homemade vs. individually packaged snacks? Will your favorite donut place put donuts in your container instead of a takeout container?

Look into the feasibility of having holiday parties catered by a local farm-to-table restaurant. You might have to take the lead ahead of time in proposing the idea and acting as a liaison between the workplace and restaurant. Consider reusable dishes from the break room rather than paper plates, plastic cups, and silverware. Round up a few of your earth-loving colleagues and volunteer for dish duty.

Encourage employees to take home leftover food from events, or donate it so it's not simply thrown away.

Chapter Seven

Fun Times: Celebrations, Gifts, and Travel

Our lives are punctuated by holidays, celebrations, and adventures—rituals that warm our hearts and create meaning and memories that carry us through the mundane everyday routines. These celebrations can be a low point for the earth in terms of the amount of waste created, so this chapter presents ways we can continue to celebrate those we love and the world we live in while honoring our connection to the earth—from holiday décor to gift-giving and green travel.

101. CREATE VALENTINES THAT SHOW YOUR LOVE FOR THE EARTH.

In the few weeks leading up to Valentine's Day, about 60 flights per day bring 15,000 tons of flowers into the United States from South America (Del Valle 2019). Just imagine the pesticides used to grow 15,000 tons of flowers and the fossil fuel waste in the gasoline to power 60 jets per day. Today, saying "I love you" on this one day of the year is a $20 billion annual industry, making it an excellent opportunity to spread some love to the earth as well as your friends and family.

INVESTMENT:

EFFORT:

TIME:

IMPACT:

Red roses are a traditional gift, but find out whether your valentine is open to a more eco-friendly option; don't just assume they want red roses. Instead look for locally grown, or at least organically grown, flowers.

If you want to give a card, look for those made from recycled paper. You can also make your own with scraps from newspaper, junk mail, magazines, and so on.

Or skip the card in favor of something else entirely. We've used a heart mold to make beeswax hearts that can hang year-round on a wall or in a window, adding beauty and natural fragrance to the air. You could also begin collecting heart-shaped rocks to paint, or write your valentine wishes on. Use your imagination to make heart-shaped cookies or heart-shaped bath bombs or heart-shaped salt or cinnamon dough ornaments.

Going out to eat? Try a local farm-to-table restaurant.

102. CHOOSE EARTH-FRIENDLY CARDS.

Every year, 2.65 billion winter holiday cards are sent in the United States, enough to fill a football field ten stories high (Peninsula Sanitary Service/Stanford Recycling Center 2020). There are other ways to fulfill this old-fashioned delight that cut down on the destruction of trees, avoid the high-gloss plastic coatings on commercial cards, and reduce the wastewater that goes into card production.

INVESTMENT:	EFFORT:
	◑
TIME:	IMPACT:
◔	

Perhaps homemade cards could be made with scraps of paper and bamboo envelopes this year, or maybe just keep it simple with e-cards. Less than $20 per year will buy you all the e-cards you could possibly want, with no stamps or addressing envelopes needed, no trees being wasted, and no fossil fuel used in transportation.

If you prefer that personal touch, look for cards made from recycled or homemade papers. You can even find cards that contain wildflower seeds in the paper, which can be planted later.

103. USE GIFT WRAP ALTERNATIVES.

Wrapping paper and gift bags can be quite beautiful, and I've long been known in my family for coordinated paper, big ribbons (that can be reused each year), and beautifully decorated packages. But each year I threw away huge amounts of wrapping paper. Annual wrapping paper waste in the United States could cover more than 5,000 football fields. It's a $9 billion industry (Intercon 2012).

INVESTMENT:	EFFORT:
	◑ - ◔
TIME:	IMPACT:
◔	

Reuse is the name of the game here. If you sew, reusable gift bags made from fabric scraps whip up quickly. If not, you can purchase them on Etsy or from some zero-waste retailers. Don't be afraid to give away gifts in them, too, encouraging people to reuse them or pass them on with another gift.

If you're looking for something more temporary, consider reusing newspapers and paper bags to wrap gifts. These gifts can be decorated with stamps, paints, kids' drawings, and more. Don't forget to reuse wrapping paper and gift bags.

To avoid plastic tape, hit up your favorite craft store for washi tape. This adhesive is made from renewable resources and comes in an assortment of prints and colors. And because it's paper, you can add it to your compost pile.

104. FAKE OR REAL? SETTLE THE HOLIDAY TREE DEBATE.

The best, most sustainable answer might depend on where you live.

INVESTMENT:

EFFORT:

TIME:

IMPACT:

I'm a fan of a real tree, grown sustainably for the occasion. I live in upstate New York, where it's not difficult to find a small farm that doesn't spray pesticides on trees. My purchase supports a local farm family and encourages planting and growth of trees.

The year I lived in Florida, that wasn't the case. I paid dearly for a half-fresh tree, trucked in from a massive producer up north and sold at my local big-box store. If this is your situation, buying a high-quality plastic tree that can be used for decades might be a better choice. Think long-term with this purchase.

Keeping a Norfolk pine as a houseplant and decorating it for the holidays is another sustainable option, as is buying a living tree that you plant after the holidays.

105. FAVOR THE EARTH WITH YOUR PARTY FAVORS.

What comes to mind when you think of party favors? I think of a small plastic bag stuffed with plastic trinkets and plastic-wrapped candies. It's easy to replace party favors with inexpensive things that benefit the earth.

INVESTMENT:

EFFORT:

TIME:

IMPACT:

For one birthday party, I had children paint clay pots and plant marigold seeds in them. It was both an inexpensive craft and a party favor. For another party, I cut out symmetrical dragonflies and glued pennies underneath them so the dragonflies would balance by the tips of their heads on a child's nose or fingers. The kids used beautiful wet-on-wet watercolor paints to decorate their dragonflies. For just a few cents, I had both a craft and a party favor.

For older kids, homemade sugar cookies that match the party's theme, chocolate-dipped strawberries, fair-trade chocolate bars, or other foods are usually popular. You could also consider movie tickets or iTunes gift cards.

For adult affairs, think of donations in lieu of favors, seed bombs, small pots of herbs or flowers, baskets of local foods, or locally made body-care products.

106. HAVE A USED HALLOWEEN.

Each year, billions of pounds of textile waste are created. Single-use, cheaply made Halloween costumes contribute, adding to the greenhouse gases that textiles emit buried in landfills. Many of the synthetic fabrics in Halloween costumes are petroleum-derived and will never decompose, adding to our microplastic pollution issue.

INVESTMENT:

EFFORT:

TIME:

IMPACT:

Consider making your own costume with items found around your house. You'll find plenty of inspiration online.

Thrift stores are wonderful places for reimagining old clothes into new characters. We've found all sorts of costumes and costume pieces there, and everything is usually quite inexpensive.

Give your own costumes a new life by donating them to a daycare center, community playgroup, children's hospital, theater, thrift store, or to friends.

What about all those individually wrapped candies? Consider choosing candies that come in boxes rather than plastic wrappers, such as Dots, Junior Mints, or Nerds. Hosting your own super cool Halloween party can also be a way to reduce this waste, trading out candy for homemade treats.

For many years, we attended a Halloween festival at a Waldorf school, a magical experience that involved very little waste and revolved around six simple but beautiful events.

» A gorgeous path was lit by hundreds of amazingly creative jack-o'-lanterns, across a field and through the woods to a little hut where the witch "Baba Yaga" handed out homemade cookies to the children.

» The jack-o'-lantern path also led to a jester, perched high off the ground, shouting down riddles to the children and tossing down candies for correct answers.

» In another spot, Mother Earth played her wooden flute and spoke softly to the children, "Oh, you're a cat! I can feel your little paws on my back. Would you like a bulb to plant in my soil?" (Flower bulbs were such a great zero-waste idea.)

» A doorway was made into an enchanted garden with little silk marionette fairies dancing among the organic lollipops "growing" in the garden.

» A puppet show in the gymnasium delighted everyone.

» A bonfire and hot apple cider rounded out the festivities. A cookie, a few candies, an organic lollipop, and a flower bulb don't generate much waste.

Whether you create your own alternative celebration or go a more traditional route, any of the steps above will keep textiles and plastics out of the landfill.

107. OFFSET YOUR TRAVEL CARBON FOOTPRINT.

Your carbon footprint is the amount of greenhouse gases your lifestyle produces in one year. Going on vacation often involves a plane flight or a long road trip, both of which generate greenhouse gas emissions.

INVESTMENT: EFFORT:

TIME: IMPACT:

CarbonFootprint.com and other companies offset greenhouse gases by planting trees, building solar panels, or engaging in other activities that reduce emissions.

How does this work? You enter your travel information into a carbon footprint calculator that determines the average amount of gases produced in a year or on a vacation. Then you're presented with options to offset this amount of greenhouse gas. These options are not free, but you may be surprised to learn that they're relatively affordable. For example, one calculator said that if I flew roundtrip from Albany, New York, to Orlando, Florida, I would generate .799 tons of CO_2, which would cost $24 to offset. I also learned that the average 11 tons of emissions produced by the average person in a developed nation could be offset for $100 to $150 annually.

108. BYO ON VACATION: LEAVE THE SINGLE-USE ITEMS FOR THE NEXT GUEST.

About two million bars of partially used hotel soap are thrown out daily in the United States, according to Clean the World, an organization that upcycles some of them for distribution in the developing world (Clean the World 2018). Untold numbers of hotel shampoo bottles and other single-use items add to daily waste. Marriott has promised to stop offering single-use toiletries in an effort to keep 500 million bottles out of landfills (Lardieri 2019).

INVESTMENT: EFFORT:

TIME: IMPACT:

Skip the single-use items entirely. Bring your own toiletries in reusable silicone travel containers. Opting for a bar soap and bar shampoo further reduces packaging and allows you to carry more shampoo, for example, than Transportation Security Agency (TSA) rules allow for liquids. Ask the hotel to take the single-use items out of your room so they don't get tossed for hygienic reasons after you leave.

Similarly, travel with a reusable water bottle and coffee mug and bring your own reusable silverware and napkins. If you're flying, the TSA requires that your bottle be empty but encourages you to fill it after you're through the checkpoint.

109. KEEP HOLIDAY DÉCOR SUSTAINABLE.

No matter which holiday(s) you celebrate, you can find ways to reduce plastics and waste, shop for local food to make holiday dishes, and buy or make eco-friendly decorations.

INVESTMENT:

EFFORT:

TIME:

IMPACT:

Thrift stores are an excellent source for holiday decorations.

Shop for locally made beeswax candles.

Make your own window decorations rather than buying plastic window clings, or shop Etsy for sustainably made decorations. Skip the blowups for the yard in favor of making decorations that wildlife can enjoy, such as birdseed treats.

Examine your annual traditions for ways to extend them to the earth. We have an annual winter solstice tradition of making gingerbread houses decorated with nuts, seeds, berries, and other healthy-for-the-animals goodies. It's so much fun watching the birds and squirrels feasting on them.

110. PLAN A TRULY HAPPY BIRTHDAY BASH.

The average American kid's birthday party costs $400 before presents (Pesce 2017). It will also generate a huge amount of waste and result in each family going home with more plastic toys.

INVESTMENT:

EFFORT:

TIME:

IMPACT:

Here are eight simple steps to a budget-friendly and sustainable birthday bash.

Choose your theme on the basis of what your child currently loves rather than what's trendy.

Choose an inexpensive venue: home, a park, or a local rec hall.

Keep décor simple and DIY. Snag a creative friend to help. Hang photos from the child's last year. Make a selfie photo booth area. Decorate your own cupcakes. Stalk Pinterest for more ideas.

Plan out the party schedule to keep things moving smoothly: snacks, game 1, craft, cake, presents, game 2.

Keep food simple and inexpensive. Don't schedule parties during mealtimes.

Ask guests to bring something meaningful in lieu of gifts: a potluck dish, a dog-shelter item, or something for a food pantry. This reduces the wrapping paper waste and plastic toys and packaging that typically pile up. Let your kid help decide what organization they want to donate to.

With all the money you've saved, you can easily afford compostable silverware and sustainably sourced paper plates and cups. Better yet, buy an inexpensive set of silverware to reuse annually.

Skip the balloons. They're a major source of environmental plastic pollution and kill countless sea and land animals and pets annually.

That's the formula for sustainable, budget-friendly birthday happiness. You'll save money while saving the environment from more plastic and paper waste.

111. NAVIGATE GIFT-GIVING WITH ZERO-WASTE GRACE.

Gift-giving can be a sensitive issue. Everyone is operating out of generosity, but not everyone is on the same zero-waste journey. I often find conflicts within parenting and zero-waste groups about how to handle holiday gift-giving with extended family. These ideas can help keep harmony in the holidays while still encouraging as much zero waste as possible.

INVESTMENT:
–

EFFORT:
◐

TIME:
🕐 - 🕐 🕐

IMPACT:

Give the family a heads-up on what your children enjoy. "If you're looking for gift-giving ideas, Ana is very into X book series." You can also put out a little PSA: "Our family is trying to reduce the amount of trash we produce after learning that 596 million pounds of waste were dumped into the earth in the first four months of 2020 alone (The World Counts 2020). We'd love to have some gift ideas for extended family that don't involve plastic or come wrapped in plastic. On our end, our kids are really loving _____."

Give the gift of experiences that will be remembered—a season pass to a favorite museum; tickets to a sporting event, concert, movie, or stage show; or a weekend camping trip with you. Equipment for hobbies also make great gifts: bikes, skis, a gift card to a dance store, or a camera, for example. You could also suggest a family experience: "If you'd like to do something memorable with the kids, they'd like to invite you to meet us for hot cocoa and cookie baking (or whatever other fun activity) on such and such date."

Give eco-friendly gifts such as local organic wine, a fair trade basket or scarf, used books, something you've handmade or that is made by local vendors, or fair trade coffee or chocolate. If you live in an area where a single big-box store is the only place to shop, consider buying online, although our popular big-box stores usually have organic fruit and fair trade chocolate that could be lovely together.

Consider asking for donations to a charity rather than gifts. "In lieu of gifts this year, our family is collecting donations for X charity."

Finally, be gracious. Some people won't get your zero-waste journey; for whatever reasons, they aren't in the same place as you. Thank them for their generosity and chill out about the wrapping paper and plastic that are out of your control. It's not our job to judge or control others. You can donate the toys later if you don't feel comfortable with plastic in your home, and you'll still be far ahead if you're only throwing out a lot of waste on holidays and birthdays, rather than all year round.

112. GOOGLE GREEN OPTIONS FOR YOUR NEXT VACATION DESTINATION.

Vacations can be expensive trips with high carbon emissions, or completely free and zero-waste adventures close to home, or anything in between. Read on for ideas to make your next vacation more sustainable for the earth.

INVESTMENT:

EFFORT:

TIME:

IMPACT:

A quick search will provide some ideas to make your next big vacation greener, from local farm-to-table restaurants to green vacation rentals. One simple step is to stay where you can depend on public transportation, or walk to local sites. Many places offer bicycle rentals.

My favorite zero-waste option? Try a staycation instead of a vacation. Stay home and plan a series of local or at-home adventures, ranging from local museums, parks, and beaches to stargazing or camping in your backyard, to exploring a new area within day-trip range. My family loves staycations; we explore new places to hike and visit small towns with coffee shops, local stores, galleries, restaurants, bookstores, consignment shops, and places to chat and people-watch. We get to sleep in our own beds and don't need to pack, make flights, or hire pet sitters. It's very inexpensive and low stress.

The best thing about a zero-waste staycation is that it's affordable for anyone. We started when I was in a low-income stage of life with just enough gas money to get us to a destination and back. We'd pack a picnic lunch and maybe scrounge up some change to buy coffee or ice cream; otherwise, we spent nothing. We looked for free things like small galleries, bookstores to browse, new parks and trails to explore, and free outdoor music. Want to be even more zero-waste? Check for things within a couple miles of you (rather than a day-trip drive) and plan a whole afternoon or day around the event.

113. WEAR WHITE BUT GO GREEN: SUSTAINABLE WEDDINGS.

Any event is an opportunity to reduce waste, and green weddings are a big trend right now. By making environmentally friendly choices, you begin your lives together with an act of kindness for the earth.

INVESTMENT:	EFFORT:
–	◐
TIME:	IMPACT:
○ ○ ○	◕ ◕

Here are seven ideas to get you started:

Shop for conflict-free diamonds or skip the diamond in favor of something truly unique. Choose rings made from fair trade and sustainably sourced materials, or go reused with a vintage item or family heirloom.

Rent a wedding gown, buy used, or shop for one made from organic textiles.

Look for local, farm-to-table catering. Just going with a cake? Fancy it up with rented plates and napkins rather than disposable.

Collaborate with a local farm, sustainability center, or composting group to compost food scraps at the reception and arrange to donate leftovers to a shelter.

Buy your flowers locally and in season. I have friends who create beautiful in-season bouquets with organically grown flowers from their farms. A Google search will help you find places to donate your flowers after the reception.

Go with eco party favors and gifts for the wedding party. A quick Google search will turn up plenty of options for every price range and interest. Some examples include a gift basket with local specialty foods, organic seed bombs (a mixture of clay and flower seeds to toss into an empty field), fair trade coffee, or reusable items like a bag or water bottle with your wedding info or a favorite quote printed on it.

Choose an eco-friendly place to hold the event—outdoor locations, refurbished barns, party tents, or hotels using sustainable energy— and consider an eco-friendly honeymoon.

114. SAY WWOOF!

World Wide Opportunities on Organic Farms (WWOOF) is an amazing way to see the world in a low-waste way that gives back to local communities and the earth.

INVESTMENT:

TIME:
🕐🕐 - 🕐🕐🕐

EFFORT:
🌑

IMPACT:

WWOOFing, as it's called, lets you trade a few hours per day of work on a farm for housing and local, often delicious food. Check the website WWOOFUSA.org for opportunities, details, and reviews of specific locations.

Each WWOOF location is different, but you might find numerous zero-waste concepts at work, such as food composting, farm-to-table meals, eco-housing, composting toilets, and sustainable agriculture. Some WWOOFers report that they've been able to help establish other zero-waste options during their stay.

While other opportunities for world travel and volunteer work exist, investigate them carefully; academic research finds that these opportunities often do more harm to communities than good by ignoring already existing resources and forcing communities to be reliant on "Western heroes" rather than their own infrastructure.

115. BOOK AN ECO-VACATION.

Whether you have a tight budget or money to splurge, a vacation doesn't have to mean abandoning your zero-waste efforts.

INVESTMENT:

TIME:
🕐🕐🕐

EFFORT:
🌓

IMPACT:

The least expensive eco-vacation would be camping or RVing in a limited geographic area. This strategy allows you to bring and cook your own zero-waste foods, reduce gasoline use, and live simply while seeing the sights.

Have money to splurge on luxury? Give some TLC to the earth in the process. Eco resorts offer a whole range of earth-loving goodness such as organic bedding and zero-carbon offsets. Many have their own farm-to-table restaurants or their own organic gardens. You might find power generated on-site, on-site water treatment, or on-site animal rescues.

These resorts are often heavily invested in their local ecosystem and local economy. You can adventure and learn about ocean life, jungle life, local wildlife, and so on. Expect to have experiences in nature such as zip-lining, yoga, and meditation. Some eco resorts offer volunteer hours in exchange for a reduced nightly cost.

Additionally, these resorts are usually quite conscious about reducing, reusing, and recycling and are often meticulous about waste that goes into air and water. You'll probably be asked to leave all chemical fragrances at home; some ask that you only use the all-natural toiletries they provide. Expect to see other rules designed to diminish toxic waste, such as removing shoes indoors and avoiding smoking on the premises.

Chapter Eight

Family Life: Kid Stuff

Children are the future of our world and our most valuable assets. Not only can we raise them with (almost) zero waste, we can also teach them to love and care for the earth, too.

Sadly, marketing to children, a multi-billion-dollar industry, leads to massive amounts of waste. Our ancestors managed to keep our evolutionary line going for millions of years with no baby showers or baby stores and no specialty kid foods. Nobody is denying that modern inventions have made our lives easier in many ways, but consumerism has become excessive, and our children can live richly without it.

In this chapter, we'll explore how to teach our children to care for the environment, how to help them understand wants versus needs, and how to live richly without falling prey to a consumer culture that creates an excess of waste.

116. TEACH KIDS TO LOVE THE EARTH WITH STORIES ASSOCIATED WITH THE SEASONS.

Educators and environmentalists tell us that by modeling a love of and joy in the earth, we create a generation of children who will be more on board with zero-waste decisions.

INVESTMENT:

EFFORT:

TIME:

IMPACT:

Want to raise future environmentalists? Help them fall in love with the earth long before they ever learn that it's in danger. When my daughter was little, one of our biggest joys each season was putting the last season's books away and bringing out the new season's stories. Libraries, of course, are wonderful if you don't want to build your own collection.

Summer stories were about gardens and fairies and local farms. Autumn books explored themes of the harvest, pumpkins, apple picking, autumn poetry, animals' preparations for winter, and gratitude. Winter books told stories of snow and hibernation. Spring books told stories about baby animals.

Year after year, my daughter learned about the seasons through her books and forays outside to observe what we were reading about. She learned how people used to live off the land, about wild edibles, and about the birds and animals in our community.

As my daughter grew, nature-loving chapter books became popular: the Herb Fairies series, which teaches children about plant medicine; *Gaia Girls*, about girls with superpowers related to earth, air, fire, or water; and classics like *My Side of the Mountain*. Your kid doesn't have to be a big reader to be inspired by nature stories. I often read aloud, and we listened to audiobooks in the car.

117. FEED BABY WITH ZERO WASTE.

Feeding our infants is very personal and all approaches can move toward sustainability.

INVESTMENT:

EFFORT:

TIME:

IMPACT:

Breastfeeding is as zero-waste as it gets, and it has many health and bonding benefits. For support, seek out your local La Leche League group and a certified lactation consultant before you give birth.

If you're among the women who can't breastfeed for physical or mental health reasons, or who choose not to, look for an organic formula, glass baby bottles, and non-plastic nipples.

As your baby grows, look into child-led weaning and homemade baby foods and snacks rather than purchasing less healthy snacks in plastic packages. Until recently, older infants and toddlers around the world ate mashed-up bits of whatever the rest of the family was eating. There's no better way to get your kids used to whole foods and the flavors you cook with. Jarred baby foods are overcooked and bland, and infant and toddler snacks are often highly processed, with too much sugar. "Kid-friendly" foods and "children's meals" are not a thing. We think they are because of the billions of dollars spent marketing them to us annually.

118. LIMIT THE NUMBER OF TOYS CHILDREN HAVE WHILE LIVING A LIFE OF ABUNDANCE.

We've forgotten the beauty in simplicity and often stretch our kids to the limits, scheduling their time with more activities than they feel comfortable with and filling our homes with more toys than they can enjoy. The truth? We can live simply while living richly.

The key is creating abundance in our lives that doesn't decrease the earth's abundance.

INVESTMENT:

EFFORT:

TIME:

IMPACT:

Choose open-ended toys that can be used in multiple ways.

Choose high-quality toys that will last and can be passed on.

If you notice your kids aren't using certain items, pack them up in a bin and store them away; they'll be new and exciting again in a few months.

No need to deprive your children. Spoil them with experiences and adventures over consumption.

119. TEACH KIDS TO BE SMARTER THAN MARKETERS.

The American Psychological Association reports that more than $12 billion is spent annually to market items to children and that the average child views some 40,000 commercials per year (APA 2004). Consequently, consumer brand and product allegiance starts around two to three years of age (Valkenburg and Buijzen 2005).

INVESTMENT:

EFFORT:

TIME:

IMPACT:

When my daughter was three years old, she had a favorite story she'd ask me to tell her when we shopped: "Mommy, tell me the story about being trickier than the tricky marketers!" The story was about discerning what we really need and saying "no" to the cultural pressure to keep up with the neighbors' buying. Telling this story with dramatic voices is pretty fun.

As children get a bit older, watch documentaries together or provide them with simple, age-appropriate explanations of how things are produced and the impact they have on our planet's waste crisis. Don't be a killjoy, though. I fully believe in living a life of abundance. What is it your child loves about a certain item? How can you re-create it in another way? Maybe they just loved it because it has a cute kitty on it. How about getting a cute kitty cookie cutter or pancake mold, or finding a beautiful kitten picture online and printing it to hang in their room?

As kids grow, peer pressure sets in. This should be taken seriously. Teach kids to feel confident in their choices and individuality, but recognize when their mental health is worth making a purchase, too.

120. BEFRIEND USED BOOKS.

INVESTMENT:

EFFORT:

TIME:

IMPACT:

Libraries, thrift stores, used bookstores, and audio books all reduce consumption of trees. Have college kids? You can save a lot of money by purchasing a slightly older edition of textbooks. There's a chance they'll be running to the college bookstore or begging off a classmate if a chapter is out of order, but with several degrees under my belt, I've yet to have this method backfire on me—though I'm guessing it works better for social sciences and the humanities than for math or science fields.

Donate books when you're done with them, or create a little community library box in front of your home.

121. MAKE ZERO WASTE COOL BUT DON'T FORCE IT.

INVESTMENT:

EFFORT:

TIME:

IMPACT:

Connect your older elementary school child or teen with other teens working toward zero waste and climate change. Today's youth tend to be very concerned about global climate change and our future. While many of them admire teenage activist Greta Thunberg, most feel she's somewhat out of their reach. Connect them online with more relatable teens who are working toward a zero-waste lifestyle. A quick YouTube search will turn up plenty of results.

Hold space for your teen to be zero waste, but don't force it. Help them host a clothing swap. Sign them up for a mechanics class, sewing class, upcycled clothing class, or something else that will help them reduce and reuse. Bring them to high-end thrift stores where they can find fashionable clothing on the cheap. Help them host a trail or roadside cleanup with friends.

Some of these ideas will work better in the later elementary and early middle-school years before the pressures of teen life become too big. Ultimately, respect your teen and be willing to make some compromises. If they say "no," don't push it. Just keep modeling and facilitating the zero-waste lifestyle as much as possible while also respecting where they are. They'll return to it later when they have more emotional space in their life. You're sacrificing some short-term zero waste for long-term connection, respect, and mental health, which ultimately are the path to passing on your values.

122. USE SEASONAL RITUALS TO CONNECT KIDS TO THE EARTH.

Simply reading about nature isn't enough. Social science research tells us that when people feel more connected to the environment, they're more likely to make eco-friendly decisions throughout their lives. The first step in raising zero-waste citizens is helping children fall in love with the earth. Otherwise, they don't know or care about what they're saving. Find ways to get your kids into nature on a regular basis. Don't discourage them from getting dirty; a dirty, muddy, wet child is a child who's had a good day.

INVESTMENT:

EFFORT:

TIME:

IMPACT:

As a young mother I was inspired by the book *Heaven on Earth,* by Sharifa Oppenheimer, to find ways to mark and celebrate the circle of the seasons in order to encourage a love of the earth. Many of the things we started then remain beloved seasonal traditions with my teenager: attending seasonal festivals, going on seasonal foraging walks, picking apples and berries, planting pots or gardens, feeding birds, making seed collages in autumn, collecting leaves, picking wildflowers, and more. Just this week, my teenage daughter cooked dandelion blossoms for dinner and picked violets for salads.

Consider starting daily walks when children are little. Let them meander and collect rocks, sticks, dandelions, and so on. Build this into a short 10- to 15-minute walk after evening meals, or to and from their school, if feasible. Add in a weekend visit to a park, or a monthly hike, or a day at a lake or ocean. The point is to keep nature in your family routines. Meanwhile, you'll be bonding over low-cost, fun family traditions.

123. PARE DOWN THE BABY GEAR.

Humans have been around for millennia, but we suddenly need huge stores to prepare for having a baby. What's essential and what's not?

INVESTMENT:

EFFORT:

TIME:

IMPACT:

A car seat is essential. However, like new cars, car seats off-gas some pretty toxic chemicals from plastics, foams, and flame retardants. Fortunately, manufacturers are becoming more aware of this issue. Check out The Gentle Nursery website for tests and safety ratings of car seats (Moussa 2020). Then let your car seat air out in the garage for a few months before using it.

Don't forget thrift stores and garage sales. They have just about every baby item you could ever want.

Baby products are a multi-billion-dollar business, but plenty of new parents purchase very little for their babies. Diapers, clothing, a car seat, a place to sleep, nail clippers and mittens, burp cloths, a teething toy and a rattle, a baby carrier, and some story books are about all that's truly needed.

As babies grow, look for blocks and other simple toys that can be used imaginatively in multiple ways. Battery-operated toys might seem exciting at first, but they are more likely to break and to short-circuit kids' imaginations. Google "open-ended toys" or "Waldorf toys" for fun ideas.

124. MODEL AND TEACH CONSCIOUS CONSUMPTION.

As kids grow, values at home come in conflict with values of the wider culture and peers. The more your child is in contact with mainstream culture, the more challenging this disconnect can become. A willingness to make some carefully thought-out compromises can go a long way toward keeping older kids and teens on board with an (almost) zero-waste lifestyle.

INVESTMENT:

EFFORT:

TIME:

IMPACT:

Don't judge, but rather listen to and validate your child's desires. Express your concerns gently. Listen more. Be willing to compromise. Ask your child how you could meet their desires while reducing, reusing, or recycling. In other words, what's the plan for how the desired items will be cared for and what's the plan for their life after your child is done with them?

As my daughter grew older, we always talked about how items were made and their impact on workers and the earth. We decided together that while it was best to avoid plastic entirely, we would be okay with a little bit of it as long as we had a plan to keep it out of a landfill. Legos provided countless hours of fun. Dolls from a popular TV show were another hit. My daughter knew, however, that we weren't going to purchase every trend; that aside from Legos, ultimately our plastic purchases would be rare and limited. We created a feeling of abundance rather than lack by focusing our attention on experiences and more sustainable toys. Allowing a few special plastic items kept her in touch with peers and culture in an important way.

125. HOST A CHILDREN'S CLOTHING/SCHOOL/TOY SWAP.

Swaps are an excellent way to embody the value of reusing—ultimately reducing our consumption and all the waste that goes into manufacturing.

INVESTMENT:

EFFORT:
◖ – ◖

TIME:
🕐🕐

IMPACT:
♻ ♻

Have friends with children a bit older or younger than yours? You could host a swap. You can make it specific to one type of item, such as clothing or school supplies, or you can extend it to any children's things at all, from furniture to sports equipment and so on.

Imagine if your kid could get a new-to-them backpack, three-ring binder, and lunch carrier simply by trading in their own. Imagine if they could pass on their bicycle to someone smaller while getting one in a larger size.

Be specific in your swap plans. You might want to host a private Facebook group where people can post freebies regularly, or you might want to host an event every six months at home or in a park. Let people know what specific items the swap is for. Set limits such as no stained items, or that items must be clean and in working order. Ask guests to bring items in reusable bags or boxes rather than plastic bags. Have a plan for displaying the items in an organized way.

Set out a snack (ask guests to contribute if you like) and let guests browse and "shop."

126. CHOOSE ALTERNATIVES TO PLASTIC TOYS.

This one can be difficult, considering how much marketing is aimed at children. Research shows that toys with limited uses don't allow children the full enjoyment of their imagination (Shrier 2016). Battery-operated plastic toys also tend to break and end up in a landfill pretty quickly. By choosing alternatives to plastic, you can reduce manufacturing waste and fossil fuel use and invest in classic, open-ended toys that can be reused for generations to come.

INVESTMENT:

EFFORT:

TIME:

IMPACT:

Look for toys made from wood, cloth, metal, and rubber. Buy used wooden blocks. Collect baskets of pine cones, seashells, or stones. Put colored scraps of cloth in another basket. My daughter used these materials, along with wood blocks and farm animals, to create huge worlds that entertained her for hours. Stones became rock walls and tables. Pine cones might be money or trees. A blue cloth might be a pond, and a green cloth a field. Later, the same green cloth might be the roof over a play picnic area or a blanket to wrap a stuffed animal in.

If your kid ends up with a lot of toys, consider putting some items in storage and pulling them out a few months later.

As a parent, I love to spoil my kid. Nature is abundant, and my zero-waste habits don't mean we feel deprived. When it came to toy purchases, we focused on quality, not quantity. Most of them remained in excellent condition despite years of play. These toys that my daughter played with throughout her toddler and elementary school years were either sold or carefully packed away to pass on to future generations.

127. CHOOSE CLOTH DIAPERS.

Did you know that a single disposable diaper takes 500 years to decompose? Using cloth diapers will save money in the long run and reduce waste. Reusable cloth wipes also keep waste out of landfills.

INVESTMENT:

EFFORT:
◑

TIME:
🕐

IMPACT:

You can invest in expensive diaper stashes, buy used ones, or check around for hand-me-downs from friends.

Diapers take a good deal of water to wash. Hanging them in the sunshine to dry helps get them extra clean and reduces use of electricity or gas for drying.

Consider elimination communication and early potty learning (not forced training). For example, it's usually pretty obvious when a six- to eight-month-old baby is having a bowel movement. Sit them on a potty and make a big deal of what comes out. The sooner children start going on the toilet, the sooner you reduce use of water for washing diapers.

You don't have to buy a plastic potty-training toilet, though I admit that a bedside potty was really nice for late night, half-asleep use when my daughter was very young and potty-learning. Many babies are fine with being held to use a full-sized toilet. You can also find old-fashioned wood toilets with metal bowls. Finally, ask friends for a hand-me-down potty.

128. CREATE ZERO-WASTE VERSIONS OF YOUR TEENS' FAVORITE FOODS.

Even the healthiest zero-waste teens enjoy popular foods like pizza, mac and cheese, chips, and soda. Needless to say, these usually come in a whole lot of packaging.

INVESTMENT:

EFFORT:

TIME:

IMPACT:

Plan a monthly cooking day. Your teen might like to join you, or not—either way is okay. If zero waste is important to you, it's your responsibility to model it, not force it. Stock up on zero-waste versions of your teen's favorite foods. For example, make some pizza crusts to store in the freezer and be sure to have DIY pizza ingredients on hand. Make homemade mac and cheese and freeze it. Freeze brownies or cookies. Buy a soda water machine and make your own fizzy drinks. Buy candies from bulk bins.

With a freezer and pantry prepped for quick zero-waste teen party foods, you'll be known as the home where everyone wants to hang out. Even if a few chip bags and takeout containers come into your home, you'll have greatly reduced waste in other ways. Your teen will appreciate that you have good food for them and their friends, even if they don't mention it now. Someday you'll see them passing on these same values in their own family.

129. TEACH KIDS FIX-IT SKILLS.

Maximizing a kid's abilities to reuse is an important life skill, and most kids are super curious about these things, especially when they're younger.

INVESTMENT:

EFFORT:

TIME:

IMPACT:

First, model the need to care for and maintain things. If you're grumpy about chores, your kids will be, too. Model an attitude of joy in caring for your home and possessions. Make chores fun.

Next, let kids help you fix the lawn mower, mend the clothing, repair the car, repurpose old items into rags, and so on. Most young children can handle tools, scissors, and sewing needles if closely supervised. Don't know how to fix things? Maybe you can share the learning process with your kids. Your chores and repairs might take longer, but you'll be spending time with your child and passing on important life skills. Ultimately, you'll be helping them reduce waste in the future and hopefully start a trend of each generation teaching these skills to the next.

130. GO BACK-TO-SCHOOL SHOPPING.

By some estimates, we throw away 1.6 billion pens each year in the United States. With all the money you saved by hosting a swap, you can invest in a few more sustainable school supplies and still come out ahead.

INVESTMENT:

EFFORT:

TIME:

IMPACT:

Shop online for pens and pencils made from recycled paper, certified sustainable wood sources, corn, recycled newspaper, or water bottles; inkless pens; refillable bamboo pens; or fountain pens. Pencil highlighters further cut down plastic waste.

Opt for paper folders rather than plastic. Decomposition and other brands make recycled paper notebooks with many fun themes on the covers. You can also find a good deal of tree-free papers.

Instead of opting for a new plastic binder annually, invest in a Naked Binder. They're made from postconsumer waste from Forest Stewardship Council–certified sustainable board. Look online for ways to decorate them and make them uniquely your own.

Chapter Nine

Consuming Consciously: Considering What and How You Buy

Earlier chapters were about the actions of (almost) zero waste. If you've read them in order, you've probably found that your mindset around consumption and your lifestyle choices has begun to shift. But you might be faced with a number of questions, still, when it comes to making purchases. This chapter addresses the thought processes behind making (almost) zero-waste purchases and seeking inspiration from overall paradigm shifts—the mindsets that will help you evaluate what decisions are best in a multitude of purchasing situations that might not be described in this book.

131. THINK NO PLASTIC.

INVESTMENT:

EFFORT:

TIME:

IMPACT:

Any time you're making a purchase and must choose between a plastic item and a non-plastic one, the non-plastic item is the better choice. There was no depletion of fossil fuels in its production, no air and water pollution from plastic manufacturing, and the afterlife of the product is better than microplastics that last eternally in our environment.

The exception is some of the newer eco-plastics that are still not widely in circulation. If you're looking at eco-plastics, consider the amount of pesticides used in their production and keep in mind that GMOs have been found to use more chemicals, not fewer (Hoffman 2013).

Occasionally you will still need to buy plastic items. I store off-season clothing in plastic bins to protect it from the occasional mice that get in. There is no getting away from plastic in our vehicles, children's car seats, or refrigerators, but the more we can reduce our use of plastics as a whole, the better off our planet will be.

132. THINK NO PACKAGING.

INVESTMENT:

EFFORT:

TIME:

IMPACT:

As a whole, items purchased with zero packaging are preferable to items that come with packaging waste. Packaging waste can be reduced by choosing loose produce and food items in bulk.

Buying used items rather than new ones also cuts down on packaging waste.

Finally, don't be afraid to complain to companies about the waste involved in shipping their goods. When enough complaints come in, companies change their habits.

133. THINK REDUCED PURCHASES.

INVESTMENT:

EFFORT:

TIME:

IMPACT:

The easiest way to reduce waste is to reduce consumption. The less we buy and the more simply we live, the less waste we produce. Keeping up with the Joneses has been the American way, but more and more Americans are following the better example of Marie Kondo. Embrace a bit of positive peer pressure and reduce what you buy. Give things away. Embrace the joys of simplicity.

It's very important to realize this doesn't mean being deprived. The key is thinking of abundance not in terms of possessions, but in terms of joy. Think about experiences over toys and high-quality sustainable items over loads of cheaper, poorly made items. Keeping kids focused on joy is a vital way to help them reduce their consumption in the midst of a consumer-driven culture. This happens not by forcing them to go without and scolding them for not being grateful, but by creating a life for them that they find full of joy. And guess what? We adults are no different. Focus on what you love. Focus on loving the earth. You'll find abundance and joy no matter what your budget, and with far less consumerism.

134. THINK USED PURCHASES.

INVESTMENT:

EFFORT:

TIME:

IMPACT:

Buying used is a major paradigm shift for going almost zero waste. You reduce the manufacturing waste that goes into new things, reduce the packaging around new items, and keep old items out of landfills.

Anytime you need a "new" item, think about where you can source it used instead. Facebook Marketplace, eBay, swaps with friends, charity shops, Craigslist, Freecycle, and your local Buy Nothing Project are all great ways to find used items free or cheap.

135. THINK LOCAL.

INVESTMENT:

EFFORT:

TIME:

IMPACT:

Locally sourced items support small businesses and keep money in the local economy. They greatly reduce the fossil fuels that go into shipping, and small local business owners are often more concerned about sustainability as a whole. (Bonus points if the business sources their goods locally.) Small businesses will often skip packaging, and local restaurants are usually open to you bringing your own takeout containers.

Locally sourced produce and farmers' market items reduce fossil fuels for shipping and are often grown in sustainable ways.

136. THINK ORGANIC FOODS.

INVESTMENT:

EFFORT:

TIME:

IMPACT:

Organic foods reduce the amount of pesticides and herbicides that go into the air, the water, and farm workers' lungs. They can be more expensive than nonorganic foods. Try shopping at Aldi, Trader Joe's, and farmers' markets to reduce costs. Sign up for an urban CSA or grow your own food.

Remember, many small farms can't afford organic certification. Don't be afraid to ask about their growing practices. In some cases, farmers go above and beyond organic certification standards with regenerative agricultural practices. Any farmer should be happy to answer specific questions on how their foods are grown. If they are hesitant or annoyed, they have something to hide. Transparency is a good sign.

137. THINK NATURAL OR RECYCLED FIBERS FOR NEW PURCHASES.

INVESTMENT:

EFFORT:

TIME:

IMPACT:

When you need to purchase new clothing, look for natural fibers over synthetics that are made from fossil fuels and, like plastics, don't really decompose. Purchase wool from well-cared-for animals or synthetics made from things like recycled plastic water bottles.

If you have money to splurge, check out some of the new vegan eco-leathers made from things like pineapple and mushrooms.

For major purchases like winter coats and ski pants, purchase high-quality items that will last for years or can be passed on to other children.

In a summery climate, items like bathing suits can be purchased from retailers that make them from recycled water bottles.

Used clothing is a simple solution here, but sometimes we all like or need something that's new. Many eco-clothing retailers are quite expensive, reflecting the true cost of clothing made without sweat-shop and factory-farm conditions. However, if you're a bargain hunter, they often have excellent sales. Try Pact Organic, Blue Canoe, Hanna Andersson, or Kate Quinn.

138. THINK OUTSIDE OF YOUR NORMAL RETAILERS.

INVESTMENT:

EFFORT:

TIME:

IMPACT:

Many sustainable (almost) zero-waste items can be purchased where you do your normal shopping, but sometimes major lifestyle changes mean changing your shopping habits, too.

Keep it simple. Identify one local (or semi-local depending on how rurally you live) sustainable retailer if you can. Maybe you want to shop there instead of your regular store, or maybe you want to add in a monthly trip. Another option is to look for an online zero-waste retailer. Shift your habits gradually to support more sustainable shopping.

In the same way, be adventurous with trying new takeout, coffee shops, or farm-to-table restaurants that support local foods. Check out farmers' markets, CSAs, and direct-from-farm purchases.

139. THINK REUSABLE.

INVESTMENT:

EFFORT:

TIME:

IMPACT:

Reusable bags, reusable straws, bulk food containers, reusable coffee mugs and water bottles, reusable silverware—you might want to keep a little basket or bag in your car, office, or school locker with a stash of reusables.

Think reusable at home: napkins, un-paper towels (the fancy name for cloth rags), makeup remover wipes, wraps for leftover food, and so forth. The more you can think of reusable items to replace single-use items, the more waste you will reduce.

140. THINK OF PRODUCT AFTERLIFE.

INVESTMENT:

EFFORT:

TIME:

IMPACT:

The ultimate goal of zero waste is that all we consume would produce compostable waste that nourishes the earth. That's a big undertaking, and we'll need to work toward it one step at a time. Composting our food scraps is a good first step. Farmer friends of mine sell their microgreens in compostable plastic bags. My local food co-op offers compostable straws and silverware for takeout. Reusable is better, of course, because there's less manufacturing waste involved, but the idea is to consider the afterlife of your purchases. It's a good idea to do an online search to determine whether an item is biodegradable and how long it takes to break down in a landfill.

141. THINK OUTSIDE OF TRENDS.

INVESTMENT:

EFFORT:

TIME:

IMPACT:

Classic clothing and toys that can be used in multiple ways will last longer than trendy items. For example, a cartoon character–based, battery-operated toy may have appeal only so long as the story that inspired it has appeal. The uses of a generic stuffed animal or doll are limited only by imagination and hence may have comparatively longer-lasting appeal.

If you really desire something trendy, shop used when possible. Help kids care for trendy toys so they can be passed on. Pair purchases of trendy clothing with wardrobe items that will last the test of time, both in terms of quality and style.

142. THINK RECYCLABLE.

INVESTMENT:

EFFORT:

TIME:

IMPACT:

Reducing and reusing are far better options than recycling, especially since many recyclable objects end up in incinerators or landfills due to high recycling costs. But if the choice is between recyclable and non-recyclable, recycling is always a better option.

143. THINK OF YOUR CARBON FOOTPRINT.

INVESTMENT:

EFFORT:

TIME:

IMPACT:

The classic way to measure individual impact on the earth is in terms of one's carbon footprint, or the amount of carbon-based emissions we create annually. You can find various carbon footprint calculators online. You can measure your annual output, the output for a trip, or the output of your business. My favorite is FootprintCalculator.org, which asks you a series of questions and then tells you how many earths we'd need if everyone in the world lived as you do. Being aware of your impact on the earth and ways to offset it helps reduce climate change waste.

144. THINK FAIR TRADE.

INVESTMENT:

EFFORT:

TIME:

IMPACT:

Fair-trade purchases are a wonderful way to ensure that imported items meet sustainability standards, provide living wages for local workers, and do not destroy local ecosystems worldwide.

Some of our beloved items like coffee and chocolate, for example, are responsible for habitat destruction due to deforestation, contaminated water, animal extinction, and child labor because of high demand for cheap products. Buying fair trade ensures that this waste does not occur.

Other fair trade items make goods by upcycling resources like metal scraps or sari silk scraps. Fair trade companies often work with disadvantaged populations. You can purchase pajamas, for example, made from sari scraps, sewn by women who were victims of sex slavery. You can purchase woven items from women in the Andes Mountains who might otherwise not have an income.

145. THINK LOVE, NOT FEAR.

INVESTMENT:	EFFORT:
TIME:	IMPACT:

It's easy to get wrapped up in fear over the fragile condition of our earth, climate change disasters, and refugees. It's easy to get consumed by fear in every choice we make, worrying about what impact we have, too afraid of our choices to live as fully as we could.

The key here, as hippie-dippie as it might sound, is love. Instead of focusing your attention on how bad things are, focus your attention on the world you're helping transform. Envision the world that your choices will create for future generations. Make your decisions out of love for yourself, love for animals, love for farm workers, and love for the earth. Let this love guide you toward joy-based decisions instead of stress-based decisions.

Chapter Ten

Big Steps: Spreading Change

We've seen that the collective power of individual choices creates real change. Just imagine, then, how powerful community-wide efforts can be. When communities around the nation take steps to reduce waste, our cultural norms begin to shift. Sustainability becomes commonplace. Some of the steps here involve more time and organization, but there are also some simple, quick steps you can take to positively impact your community.

146. COORDINATE A COMMUNITY-WIDE EDUCATIONAL PROGRAM.

Some zero-waste steps are super simple, like purchasing a reusable water bottle. Others require some education, such as composting, growing your own food, and canning or fermenting your harvest for long-term winter storage. While the Internet is full of information, there can be information overload. Sometimes it's really nice to learn in a group with others and have someone to whom you can ask questions directly.

INVESTMENT:

EFFORT:

TIME:

IMPACT:

Host an (almost) zero-waste sustainability program at your local library, community center, religious center, or school. You can teach classes or coordinate with other community experts. Offer a monthly drop-in series, each month focusing on a different topic. A four-week series or a weekend workshop could go more in-depth on a single topic.

Educating your community provides a platform for questions and discussion. (My city has a zero-waste Facebook group.)

147. CREATE A GIFT ECONOMY.

We've all heard "nothing in life is free." But what if things *were* free?

INVESTMENT:

EFFORT:

TIME:

IMPACT:

In a gift economy, people don't barter, trade, or pay for items. They simply gift them, creating an excellent means to embody the zero-waste ideas of reducing and reusing. One of the best examples of a zero-waste gift economy is the Buy Nothing Project, a community-based organization with a focus on giving, asking, and gratitude. Check out the Buy Nothing Project website to see if there's a chapter in your locality.

You might also want to take the values of the Buy Nothing Project and adapt them to create a gift economy in your business, school, or other community group.

148. CREATE COMMUNITY COMPOST.

Organic matter, such as food and yard waste, needs oxygen to decompose—an element not available in landfills. In dumps, it creates methane gas, one of the more harmful climate change emissions. According to ClimateCentral.org, if food waste emissions were a nation, it would be the third largest producer of climate change emissions, ranking just after the United States and China (Kirby 2013). Composting provides a viable solution to this dilemma.

INVESTMENT:

EFFORT:

TIME:

IMPACT:

One of the easiest ways to create a community compost service on a small-community scale is to work in conjunction with your local farmers' market. Ask farmers if they'd be willing to put out a bin to collect compost. Many are happy for extra scraps to build their soil. Similarly, community gardens are often happy to collect compost.

If you want to compost on a larger scale, the Institute for Local Self-Reliance (ILSR) notes that while 58 percent of all yard waste is composted, less than 5 percent of food waste in the United States is composted (Platt, McSweeney, and Davis, 2014). In both categories, there's huge room for improvement. ILSR provides a free 120-page PDF just on the topic of city-wide composting: ILSR.org/wp-content /uploads/2014/07/growing-local-fertility.pdf.

149. CONNECT PEOPLE TO BIOREGIONAL FOODS.

Food and other items we purchase are seldom produced right in our own communities, so much so that we are often ignorant of the value in our local bioregion. Webster's defines a bioregion as "a region whose limits are naturally defined by topographic and biological features (such as mountain ranges and ecosystems)." When we source local foods from within a 100-mile radius, for example, we're focusing on foods from our local bioregion. Bioregional goods reduce fossil fuel depletion from shipping and often result in less chemical waste in our environment due to the simple fact that native plant species are ideally suited to local growing conditions. How do you build this connection?

INVESTMENT:

EFFORT:

TIME:

IMPACT:

First, be a liaison to build relationships between local farmers and local restaurants. Take farmers' supply lists with prices to restaurants and request that the restaurant create some local dishes. Remember, starting small is always the key; encourage restaurants to feature one weekly special that is based on organic, seasonal, local foods. If the special is a hit, they'll certainly consider adding more local foods to the menu.

Second, host a plant walk to learn about wild edibles and medicinal plants in your region. Contact local herbalists, botanists, or wilderness/forest school teachers to lead the walk. A large park or farm is a great place to host it. People might be surprised to find edibles right in their backyards. For example, in New York State, wild garlic mustard is an invasive species whose roots destroy plants native to the ecosystem. Yet the garlic mustard leaves are one of the most nutritious greens in existence. Those of us "in the know" use it for salads, sautéed greens, pesto, and more. We're creating less waste by not purchasing greens shipped long distances while also helping protect our local eco-system. Similarly, Japanese knotweed is another invasive species here, but it is one of the primary herbs used to treat Lyme disease, which has also invaded this region.

Third, consider hosting a bioregional potluck. The rule? All foods must be sourced from within a 100- or 200-mile radius. Post a flyer at the event or give a brief talk on foods that are and are not native to the region. Use this as an opportunity to connect people with farmers, CSAs, and local herbalists by asking each person to note where the food items in each dish came from. You can also ask farmers and herbalists to give a brief talk at the potluck. By teaching others about local food availability and hosting a potluck, you encourage people to shop local and demonstrate delicious ways to use "strange" local foods like kohlrabi or celeriac. Again, this reduces fossil fuel waste from shipping and the other waste created in factory-farm systems.

150. ASK YOUR SCHOOL OR BUSINESS TO CHANGE.

Chapter 6 is full of ideas for instituting changes in the workplace or school environment. Your HR department, management, and school professionals are already busy with work responsibilities, so an emotional appeal that feels like it will require more work is not going to be effective. Here are three steps to create an appeal for change that will get attention.

INVESTMENT:

EFFORT:
◑

TIME:
🕐 🕐 🕐

IMPACT:

First, do your homework. Be factual and succinct, and use reliable sources of information. The World Counts website is a great resource. Use the wording below and adjust it to your topic of choice. You'll want to focus on the problem, the solution, and the benefits. Your problem should share brief, reliable facts. Your solution should be clear and easy to implement, and your benefits should focus not just on the environmental impact but also on company profits.

The Problem: According to Record Nations, the average office worker uses 10,000 sheets of copy paper annually, and more than 65 billion sheets of paper are used daily in the United States (O'Mara 2020). This is enough paper to make a 12-foot-high wall extending from New York to California (The World Counts 2020). This is problematic because "pulp and paper is the third largest industrial polluter of air, water, and soil" (The World Counts 2020). Paper production also contributes to deforestation, which contributes to a sizable portion of our greenhouse gas emissions and destroys ecosystems in developing nations (Harrison, et al. n.d.).

The Solution: We can reduce paper use in these ways:

» Use digital-emailed notes for meetings instead of printed handouts.

» Encourage office-wide emails rather than written memos.

» Make only one copy when we need handouts at meetings and pass it around for people to take a photo on their phone for reference.

» Print on both sides of paper.

» Make use of scrap paper. For example, we can reuse the meeting handout that we took a photo of by saving it to print on the other side.

» Use some of the money we save on paper to purchase recycled paper.

Benefits: By reducing our paper use, we cut the waste we create, as well as from paper manufacturing. The added bonus is saving money. A study by Tufts University found that large businesses report savings of $60,000 to $1.5 billion annually simply from reduced paper use (Sarantis 2002). The same study also reported that companies noted higher production rates and more profits as a result of digitizing vs. handling printed forms.

After you've done your homework and created your own form like the one above, the second step is to present your information clearly. Whether you want to do so in an email, a PowerPoint, or a face-to-face meeting, you'll want to remain professional, succinct, and fact-based. Stick to one idea at a time (e.g., the paper example above) and create a presentation that takes no more than five minutes of your boss's time.

Finally, be willing to go the extra mile when your idea is implemented. Don't criticize when people forget; simply keep reminders where everyone can see them so people don't feel singled out. Focus on the positives and create a feeling of team effort and team victory. For example, send out an email saying, "Congratulations, everyone! Our paper use is down and we're on our way to saving trees, reducing climate change emissions, and saving our company money. Keep up the great work!" If you can use exact measures of how much paper has been reduced to make the email more impactful, do so.

By following the format above and keeping your presentation short, fact-based, and logical, you'll find it much easier to implement (almost) zero-waste changes at work or school.

151. GET POLITICALLY INVOLVED.

Grassroots individual efforts and community efforts are powerful. Ultimately, we hugely outnumber any political organization or corporation. How we vote with our dollars can create major changes. Yet it can be discouraging when those in power make decisions that result in more waste and more harm to our earth home, and when one decision on their part holds such incredible influence.

INVESTMENT:

EFFORT:
◐

TIME:
🕐 🕐 🕐

IMPACT:
◉ ◉

Time for some political involvement. First, get out and vote. Choose candidates who have a demonstrated history of making environmentally responsible choices.

Second, talk to politicians and candidates. Ask candidates their positions on relevant topics of zero waste and sustainability and pressure officials to legislate in favor of our earth home over profits.

Third, join environmental organizations, sign petitions, send letters, and make phone calls. Check out the Environmental Protection Bills link in the resources section at the back of this book. This website allows you to see all pending environmental legislation in the US Congress and provides links to walk you through how to write or call in support of sustainability. Do a quick Internet search for pending environmental legislation in your state to identify legislation you can get involved with.

152. CREATE A GARDEN-TO-CAFETERIA PROGRAM.

Garden-to-cafeteria programs partner with schools to help them grow their own food, thereby reducing waste, providing fresh and delicious in-season foods, and teaching children about food production. Sadly, the Internet is full of random surveys of kids who couldn't identify common vegetables, and I'll never forget my five-year-old neighbor who was horrified that I was eating a strawberry "from dirt." Wouldn't it be wonderful if our children could learn about healthy, zero-waste food production and why it's important?

INVESTMENT:

EFFORT:

TIME:

IMPACT:

Chef Alice Waters created one of the best-known school garden programs, The Edible Schoolyard Project, in Berkeley, California, in 1995 (Edible Schoolyard 2020). Since then, her program and many others, such as FarmToSchool.org and Whole Kids Foundation, have worked to connect children with sustainable food.

The Edible Schoolyard offers online and in-person training programs, and their website provides lesson plans to incorporate gardening, zero waste, healthy cooking/eating, and sustainability into pre-K through 8th grade curricula.

You can start small and work up to a school-wide program. For example, perhaps you and a garden-savvy parent want to start a simple 4' x 4' box garden for your child's class. You can find inspiration for lesson plans on The Edible Schoolyard website. Focus on foods that are fun for kids; for example, maybe you want to make a pizza and taco garden with cherry tomatoes, peppers, lettuce, cilantro, basil, and oregano. Or maybe you want to grow pumpkins to send home in fall for jack-o'-lanterns and pies.

153. ESTABLISH A COMMUNITY RECYCLING PROGRAM.

According to National Geographic, 91 percent of plastics are not recycled (Parker 2019). What can you do?

INVESTMENT:

EFFORT:
◍

TIME:
◍ ◍ ◍

IMPACT:
◍ ◍ ◍

First, make recycling easy. Petition your city to set up recycling bins at events. People are unlikely to carry their plastic water bottle home to recycle, but when a recycling bin stands next to the public trash bin, the right choice is easy.

Second, contact your local trash service and urge them to offer recycling as a norm.

Third, petition your legislators to create more stringent recycling laws. Recycling laws vary from state to state and even from object to object.

For example, Call2Recycle relates that some states require battery recycling, other states only require that manufacturers offer the option to recycle, and yet other states have zero battery recycling laws (Call2Recycle 2020). Similarly, The Association of Plastic Recyclers recounts that only seven states have any laws about recycling plastics (Association of Plastic Recyclers 2020).

154. HOST A GROUP CLEANUP.

Waste on our roadways and streets not only detracts from property values and neighborhood beauty, it also comes with serious environmental issues. Cigarette butts, for example, take 10 years to decompose and leach poisons like arsenic into soil and water. Other trash ends up eaten by animals, slowly killing them. Ultimately, much of the trash ends up in waterways. Additionally, research shows that when people see litter on the ground, they're more likely to litter in that area (Caucasus Environmental Knowledge Portal 2020).

INVESTMENT:

EFFORT:

TIME:

IMPACT:

Host a community cleanup. You can do this as an individual or as part of a community organization such as a school, business, fraternity or sorority, scouts, or a religious group. First, you'll need to set a date and time and advertise the event. Use zero-waste ways to advertise such as email, verbal announcements, and flyers made from scrap paper.

Next, make sure that people are safely equipped. If you live in an urban area or will have a large group, contact your local police department for advice. Everyone should wear bright, clearly visible clothing and the cleanup should occur during the day. Gloves can protect against scraps of glass and bacteria. If using disposable gloves, latex and nitrile will decompose over time, whereas plastic will not.

Arrange your group in some way to separate out trash and recyclables. You can do this by putting recycling bins in each cleanup area or by having some folks focus on trash and others on recycling.

Finally, you'll need to arrange for the trash disposal. If you're working with a business that has dumpsters, this is easy. If the community charges for trash disposal, call your local trash pickup ahead of time to make arrangements for an extra pickup. Explain that you're doing a community service project and ask if they'll donate the trash pickup as part of the project.

155. ESTABLISH A COMMUNITY GARDEN.

Many people don't live in an area where they can grow their own food. Community gardens provide a hyper-local solution. You might not have to reinvent the wheel; many areas already have community garden programs. It's possible that you'll be able to work with an existing organization to create a garden in your own neighborhood. Do an Internet search and ask around—you might be happily surprised to find you can skip some of the five steps below. In any case, these steps break down the process of creating a community garden as simply as possible.

INVESTMENT:

EFFORT:
○

TIME:
○○○

IMPACT:
●●●

First, build your team. Have a community garden meeting at your local library, food co-op, or community center. See who is interested and what skills they can bring to the team. You'll need a community liaison to find land and help advertise, a grant writer, people who can build gardens and install fences, and people who can offer customer service to members (signing them up for garden plots, taking payment, and creating their organic gardens).

Second, find land. See if your city will donate an abandoned lot or allow you to use a portion of a park. If not, identify other community businesses that might have vacant land available. Live in an apartment complex? Pass around a petition to build a community garden on their land. Purchasing land should be a last resort, unless you have funds upfront.

Third, look for grants. You'll need money to test your soil for safety and fertility, potentially to purchase more soil, to build garden beds, and to put in fencing to keep wildlife out. You might also want to build a garden shed for tool shares or a greenhouse for seed starting. Most community gardens charge members a plot-rental fee. Grants can cover this cost, allowing you to create a free, low-cost, or sliding-scale community garden if you live in one of the many food desert areas that exist as a legacy of redlining, a legal form of discrimination through the late 1970s that denied people mortgages based on skin color, ethnicity, and geographic location with no regard to income or credit score.

Fourth, build the garden and start signing up members.

Fifth, help your members be zero-waste. Encourage them to bring home their harvest in recycled boxes or reusable bags instead of plastic. Do seed starts in cardboard pots rather than plastic. (And keep those gardens organic.)

By creating community gardens you provide neighborhoods with healthy sources of local, organic, seasonal, delicious foods that are zero-waste.

Resources

Documentaries

These films cover a variety of sustainable and zero-waste living topics.

A Plastic Ocean examines how much plastic ends up in our oceans.

Bag It is the story of a man who stops using plastic bags and how this impacts his life.

Cowspiracy explores the impact animal agriculture has on the environment in terms of waste created.

Food, Inc. takes a highly educational look into our current food production methods and their impacts on people, animals, and the environment. From health to waste to more sustainable methods, this film covers it all.

Game Changers examines whether a vegan lifestyle can really provide health and strength. Is veganism only good for reducing planetary waste, or is it good for us, too?

Growing Cities looks at the growth of urban farms in the United States and how they impact our ability to produce sustainable, (almost) zero-waste food systems.

Inside the Garbage of the World discusses plastic pollution, oceans, climate change, and the future of humanity.

Minimalism tells the stories of people who have chosen simpler, more sustainable lifestyles.

No Impact Man is the story of Colin Beavan, who made radical lifestyle changes for the health of the environment.

Plastic Is Forever explores the impact of plastics and a zero-waste lifestyle.

The True Cost explores the impact of the fashion industry on people and the earth, discussing how much waste is created and how people are hurt in the process.

The World According to Monsanto provides some background history of GMO giant Monsanto, and the impact it is having on the world. Discussion centers around the massive amount of toxic waste they've put into the earth and the cancers this has caused.

Organic Clothing

H&M isn't as sustainable as most on this list, but it does make an effort to sell some basics in organic cotton: HM.com.

Hanna Andersson, a Scandinavian company, is known for their high-quality children's clothing, often in organic or OEKO-TEX certified fabrics. They also sell a limited amount of adult clothing. Matching organic family pajamas and their children's day-dress-play-dress with leggings are some of their most popular items. They are expensive but have good sales: HannaAndersson.com.

Kate Quinn makes sustainable infant and children's clothing in a variety of adorable prints and solids: ShopKateQuinn.com.

Pact is excellent for all ages with basics such as underwear, leggings, pants, T-shirts, socks, and classic-style dresses. Pact is known for their affordable prices and excellent sales: WearPact.com.

Synergy has a broad range of styles ranging from T-shirts to dressier clothing: SynergyClothing.com.

As their name suggests, tentree plants trees in exchange for purchase of their organic clothing. They feature mostly T-shirts, sweatshirts, and other comfy clothes: tentree.com

Rawganique provides organic shower curtains, blankets, rugs, clothing, and more: Rawganique.com.

Zero-Waste Retailers: These are a few of my go-to sources for purchasing package-free and plastic-free items:

> » PackageFreeShop.com

> » ZeroWasteStore.com

> » ChagrinValleySoapandSalve.com

> » ZeroWasteCartel.com

YouTube Videos

5 Easy Zero Waste Tips for Teens: This video is created by a teen for teens living at home. It covers everything from daily habits to school to talking to parents. YouTube.com/watch?v=xvtdMjpyd6Q

Food Justice Is About Everything We Do: This episode of *The Laura Flanders Show* talks about creating sustainable food systems. YouTube.com/watch?v=Zv8YJ8HMZOI

How This Activist Farmer Fights Racism Through Food: This interview with Leah Penniman on the *Today* show looks at producing zero-waste foods for food deserts. YouTube.com/watch?v=LVZq3jITD2g

Websites

Environmental Protection Bills: This website allows you to find and track bills related to protecting the environment. You can search by specific category and see the prognosis for the bills related to that topic; it also makes it easy to track the bill and call or write Congress: GovTrack.us/congress/bills/subjects/environmental_protection/6038

Environmental Working Group: The EWG gathers extensive scientific studies on the safety of products and disseminates this information for consumers. They provide databases for cleaning supplies, foods, toiletries, furniture, and more. Download the EWG app on your phone to check the safety of thousands of items easily: EWG.org

Locally Grown Food: This website connects you with local farms, farmers' markets, CSAs, and pick-your-own places in your geographic region: LocalHarvest.org

Soul Fire Farm: Author of *Farming While Black,* international speaker and farmer Leah Penniman and her family are at the forefront of bringing sustainable, low-waste food to communities impacted by systemic racism: SoulFireFarm.org

Trash Is for Tossers: This is the website of zero-waste guru Lauren Singer, who fits five years of trash into a canning jar. It's full of inspiration and tips, videos, and a store: TrashIsForTossers.com

Zero Waste Gift Economy: This is a hyper-local gift economy. Search for your area and join to give away and receive free items: BuyNothingProject.org

References

Ahmed, Sara. 2018. "Paying a Premium for 'Natural' Products? Here's What You Should Be Looking for Instead." POPSUGAR.com/beauty /What-Does-Natural-Mean-Beauty-Products-44764023.

American Rivers. n.d. "How Sewage Pollution Ends Up in Rivers." AmericanRivers.org/threats-solutions/clean-water/sewage-pollution.

Andersen, Kip, and K. Kuhn. 2014. *Cowspiracy: The Sustainability Secret.* IMDb .com/title/tt3302820.

American Psychological Association (APA). 2004. "Report of the APA Task Force on Advertising and Children." APA.org/pubs/info/reports /advertising-children.

Association of Plastic Recyclers. 2020. "Mandatory Plastic Recycling Legislation." PlasticsRecycling.org/resources/state-recycling/mandatory -plastic-recycling-legislation.

Bedosky, Lauren. 2019. "The Difference Between Chemical and Mineral Sun-screen." *Everyday Health.* EverydayHealth.com/skin-beauty/chemical-vs -mineral-sunscreen-whats-difference.

Bedwell, Sarah. 2019. "Tubeless Toothpaste Pills: Saving Our Teeth and the Planet." *Plastic Generation.* PlasticGeneration.com/tubeless-plastic-free -toothpaste.

Bello, Walden. 2013. "Twenty-Six Countries Ban GMOs. Why Won't the U.S.?" *The Nation.* TheNation.com/article/archive/twenty-six-countries-ban-gmos -why-wont-us.

Blanchard, Rick. 2018. "How to Keep Old Mattresses Out of Landfills." *Zero Waste Wisdom.* ZeroWasteWisdom.com/post/2018/03/06/how-to-keep-old -mattresses-out-of-landfills.

Blum, Arlene, et al. 2015. "The Madrid Statement on Poly and Perfluoroalkyl Substances." *Environmental Health Perspectives.* EHP.NIEHS.NIH.gov/doi/10.1289 /ehp.1509934.

Boyle, Megan and Samara Geller, 2016. "Skip the Fabric Softeners." Environmental Working Group. EWG.org/enviroblog/2016/05/skip-fabric-softeners.

Brandt-Rauf, Paul Wesley, et al. 2012. "Plastics and Carcinogenesis: The Example of Vinyl Chloride." *Journal of Carcinogenesis.* NCBI.NLM.NIH.gov/pmc /articles/PMC3327051/#!po=2.00000.

Bringslimark, Tina, Grete Grindal Patil, and Terry Hartig. 2008. "The Association Between Indoor Plants, Stress, Productivity and Sick Leave in Office Workers." *Acta Horticulturae.* 775:117–22. doi.org/10.17660/ActaHortic .2008.775.13.

Brucker, Drew. 2018. "40 Reasons to Think Differently About Your Trash: Facts, Statistics, and More." Rubicon. Rubicon.com/blog/trash-reason -statistics-facts.

Bryce, Emma. 2019. "Should You Take Off Your Shoes Indoors?" *Live Science.* LiveScience.com/64409-should-you-take-off-shoes-indoors.html.

Burchett, Margaret, Fraser Torpy, and Jane Tarran. 2010. "Greening the Great Indoors for Human Health and Wellbeing." Feb. 2010. Report NY06021. Horticulture Australia, University of Technology, Sydney.

Call2Recycle. 2020. "Explore the Secret Life of Batteries." Call2Recycle.org /explore-the-secret-life-of-batteries.

Call2Recycle. 2020. "Recycling Laws by State." Call2Recycle.org/recycling -laws-by-state.

Carbon Footprint. n.d. "Free Carbon Calculators." CarbonFootprint.com /calculator1.html.

Carrington, Damian. 2014. "Eating Less Meat Essential to Curb Climate Change, Says Report." *The Guardian.* TheGuardian.com/environment/2014/dec/03/eating -less-meat-curb-climate-change.

Caucasus Environmental Knowledge Portal. 2020. "Reasons, Consequences and Possible Solutions of Littering." Environment.CENN.org/waste -management/publications/reasons-consequences-possible-solutions -littering.

Certified Humane. 2014. "'Free Range' and 'Pasture Raised' Officially Defined by HFAC for Certified Humane® Label." CertifiedHumane.org/free-range -and-pasture-raised-officially-defined-by-hfac-for-certified-humane-label.

Casey, Allison. 2012. "Program Your Thermostat for Fall and Winter Savings." Department of Energy. Energy Saver. Energy.gov/energysaver/articles /program-your-thermostat-fall-and-winter-savings.

Clean the World. 2018. "How Clean the World Is Changing the World." CleanTheWorld.org.

Conservation International. 2020. "Deforestation: 11 Facts You Need to Know." Conservation.org/stories/11-deforestation-facts-you-need-to-know.

Cowspiracy. 2014. "The Facts." Cowspiracy.com/facts.

Dalton, Jane. 2020. "Coronavirus: Timeline of Pandemics and Other Viruses That Humans Caught by Interacting with Animals." *Independent.* Independent .co.uk/news/uk/home-news/coronavirus-pandemic-viruses-animals-bird -swine-flu-sars-mers-ebola-zika-a9483211.html.

Del Valle, Gaby. 2019. "The hidden environmental cost of Valentine's Day roses." *Vox.* Vox.com/the-goods/2019/2/12/18220984/valentines-day -flowers-roses-environmental-effects.

Denchak, Melissa. 2018. "Water Pollution: Everything You Need to Know." Natural Resources Defense Council. NRDC.org/stories/water-pollution -everything-you-need-know.

Donley, Nathan. 2016. "Does Meat Contain Pesticides?" Medium.com/ center-for-biological-diversity/does-meat-contain-pesticides-c587f6b252e7.

Downstream Project. 2019. "Take the Test: How Many Earths Do You Need?" TheDownstreamProject.org/2013/08/26/take-the-test-how-many-earths -do-you-need.

EarthTalk. 2009. "Wipe or Wash? Do Bidets Save Forest and Water Resources?" *Scientific American.* ScientificAmerican.com/article/earth -talks-bidets.

EcoWatch. 2015. "Fast Fashion Is the Second Dirtiest Industry in the World, Next to Big Oil." EcoWatch.com/fast-fashion-is-the-second-dirtiest-industry -in-the-world-next-to-big--1882083445.html.

Edible Schoolyard. 2020. "Our Story." EdibleSchoolyard.org/about.

Energy Saver. 2020. "Savings Project: Lower Water Heating Temperature." Energy.gov/energysaver/services/do-it-yourself-energy-savings-projects /savings-project-lower-water-heating.

Environment, Health and Safety Online. 2020. "Candles and Indoor Air Quality." EHSO.com/candles2.htm.

Environmental Working Group. 2019a. EWG's Healthy Living Home Guide. EWG.org/healthyhomeguide/.

———. 2019b. Mattresses. EWG's Healthy Living Home Guide. EWG.org /healthyhomeguide/mattresses.

———. 2020a. EWG's 2020 Guide to Sunscreens. EWG.org/sunscreen.

———. 2020b. Clean Fifteen: EWG's 2020 Shopper's Guide to Pesticides in Produce. EWG.org/foodnews/clean-fifteen.php.

———. 2020c. Cleaning Supplies and Your Health. EWG.org/guides/cleaners /content/cleaners_and_health.

Erskine, Eliza. 2020. "Plastic Toothbrushes Add 50 Million Pounds of Waste to Landfills Every Year!" One Green Planet. OneGreenPlanet.org/environment /plastic-toothbrushes-waste.

Expandus Ceramics. 2020. "Does Ceramic Biodegrade?" ExpandusCeramics. com/qa/does-ceramic-biodegrade.html.

Fasanella, Kaleigh. 2017. "What 'Hypoallergenic' Really Means in Cosmetics." *Allure.* Allure.com/story/what-does-hypoallergenic-mean-in-cosmetics.

Fjeld, Tove, and C. Bonnevie. 2002. "The Effect of Plants and Artificial Day-Light on the Well-Being and Health of Office Workers, School Children, and Health Care Personnel." Proceedings of Plants for People International Symposium. PlantSolutions.com/documents/PlantsArtificialDaylight.pdf.

Fjeld, Tove, et al. 1998. "The Effect of Indoor Foliage Plants on Health and Discomfort Symptoms among Office Workers." *Indoor Built Environments* 7:204–9. Journals.SAGEPub.com/doi/10.1177/1420326X9800700404.

Food and Agriculture Organization of the United Nations. n.d. Key Facts and Findings. FAO.org/news/story/en/item/197623/icode.

Formuzis, Alex. 2018. "Tests Find PFAS Chemicals in Cosmetics at 'Elevated Levels'." Environmental Working Group. EWG.org/release/tests-find-pfas -chemicals-cosmetics-elevated-levels.

Frack, Lisa, and Becky Sutton. 2010. "3,163 Ingredients Hide Behind the Word 'Fragrance'." Environmental Working Group. EWG.org/enviroblog/2010/02/31 63-ingredients-hide-behind-word-fragrance.

Global Organics. n.d. "4 Categories of Organic Product Labels." Global -Organics.com/post.php?s=2016-03-29-4-categories-of-organic-product-labels.

Gregorio, Sandy. 2018. "Hazards of Car Air Fresheners—How to Stay Safe." National Motorists Association. Motorists.org/blog/hazards-of-car-air -fresheners-how-to-stay-safe.

Harrison, Brion, Coral Mullen, James Rupinski, and Alec Schweinberg. n.d. "Entrance of Paper Mill Effluent Chemicals into Ecosystems and Their Sub-sequent Biomagnification and Interaction with Humans—A Review." *Marine Science Today.* MarineScienceToday.com/wp-content/uploads/2015/02/2-23 -EntranceofPaperMillEffluentChemicalsIntoEcosystems.pdf.

Harvard School of Public Health. 2019. "Some Dental Floss May Expose People to Harmful Chemicals." HSPH.Harvard.edu/news/hsph-in-the-news/dental -floss-harmful-chemicals.

Helmer, Jodi. 2019. "The Massive Impact of Your Takeout Coffee Cup." FoodPrint. FoodPrint.org/blog/environmental-impact-coffee-cup.

Hoffman, Beth. 2013. "GMO Crops Mean More Herbicide, Not Less." *Forbes.* Forbes.com/sites/bethhoffman/2013/07/02/gmo-crops-mean-more-herbicide -not-less/#29086ca3cd53.

Hogan, Rita. 2019. "Beware the Dangers of Undiluted Essential Oils to Your Dog." *Dogs Naturally*. DogsNaturallyMagazine.com/dangers-undiluted-essential -oils-dog.

Huber, Chris. 2017. "World's Food Waste Could Feed 2 Billion People." World Vision. worldvision.org/hunger-news-stories/food-waste.

Intercon. 2012. "Sobering Fact: Wrapping Paper Could Cover Over 5000 Football Fields." InterconGreen.com/2012/12/26/sobering-fact-wrapping -paper-could-cover-over-5000-football-fields.

Isaacs-Thomas, Isabella. 2019. "Why Your Cosmetics Don't Have to Be Tested for Safety." PBS. PBS.org/newshour/health/why-your-cosmetics-dont-have-to -be-tested-for-safety.

Jaslow, Ryan. 2011. "Scented Laundry Products Release Carcinogens, Study Finds." CBS News. CBSNews.com/news/scented-laundry-products-release -carcinogens-study-finds.

Kerlin, Kat. 2015. "Plastic for Dinner: A Quarter of Fish Sold at Markets Contain Human-Made Debris." UC Davis. UCDavis.edu/news/plastic-dinner -quarter-fish-sold-markets-contain-human-made-debris.

Kirby, Alex. 2013. "Food Waste Worsens Greenhouse Gas Emissions: FAO." Climate Central. ClimateCentral.org/news/food-waste-worsens-greenhouse -gas-emissions-fao-16498.

Kobayashi, Kent, Andrew Kaufman, John Griffis, and James McConnell. 2007. "Using Houseplants to Clean Indoor Air." Cooperative Extension Service. University of Hawai'i at Manoa. Scholarspace.manoa.hawaii.edu/bitstream /10125/2960/1/OF-39.pdf.

Kovach, Joseph, C. Petzoldt, J. Degni, and J. Tette. 1992. "A Method to Measure the Environmental Impact of Pesticides." New York's Food and Life Sciences Bulletin. Cornell University Library. eCommons.Cornell.edu/handle/1813 /55750.

Lardieri, Alexa. 2019. "Marriott to Replace Small Toiletry Bottles with Large Recyclable Ones." *U.S. News & World Report*. USNews.com/news/national

-news/articles/2019-08-28/marriott-to-replace-small-single-use-toiletry
-bottles-with-large-recyclable-ones.

Lindsey, Rebecca. 2020. "Climate Change: Atmospheric Carbon Dioxide."
Climate.gov/news-features/understanding-climate/climate-change-atmospheric
-carbon-dioxide.

Morgan, Andrew. 2015. *The True Cost*. IMDb.com/title/tt3162938.

Moussa, Yasmine. 2020. "Non-Toxic Car Seats: How to Avoid Toxic Flame
Retardants in Car Seats." The Gentle Nursery. GentleNursery.com/natural-baby
-registry-guide/non-toxic-car-seats.

Naseem, Mustafa, et al. 2020. "Oil Pulling and Importance of Traditional
Medicine in Oral Health Maintenance." *International Journal of Health Sciences*.
NCBI.NLM.NIH.gov/pmc/articles/PMC5654187.

National Geographic Resource Library. 2020. "Great Pacific Garbage Patch."
NationalGeographic.org/encyclopedia/great-pacific-garbage-patch.

Naveed, Niha. 2014. "The Perils of Cosmetics." *Journal of Pharmaceutical Sciences
and Research*. SemanticScholar.org/paper/The-Perils-of-Cosmetics-Naveed
/0b82131752fac7b61abfc9f08a7d0f55343d2d9f.

New Directions Aromatics. 2019. "Essential Oils for Your Pet: A Safety Guide."
NewDirectionsAromatics.com/blog/products/petfriendly-essential-oils.html.

Non-GMO Project. 2016. "GMO Facts." NONGMOProject.org/gmo-facts.

Occupational Health & Safety. 2018. "Study: PVC Shower Curtains Potentially
Toxic." OHSOnline.com/Articles/2008/06/Study-PVC-Shower-Curtains
-Potentially-Toxic.aspx?Page=1.

OEKO-TEX. 2020. "Our Standards." OEKO-TEX.com/en.

O'Mara, Morgan. 2020. "How Much Paper Is Used in One Day?" Record
Nations. RecordNations.com/2016/02/how-much-paper-is-used-in-one-day.

Parker, Laura. 2018a. "Straw Wars: The Fight to Rid the Oceans of Discarded
Plastic." *National Geographic*. NationalGeographic.com/news/2017/04/plastic
-straws-ocean-trash-environment.

———. 2018b. "A Whopping 91% of Plastic Isn't Recycled." *National Geographic.* NationalGeographic.com/news/2017/07/plastic-produced-recycling-waste -ocean-trash-debris-environment.

Peninsula Sanitary Service/Stanford Recycling Center. n.d. "Frequently Asked Questions: Holiday Waste Prevention." LBRE.Stanford.edu/pssistanford -recycling/frequently-asked-questions/frequently-asked-questions-holiday -waste-prevention.

Pesce, Nicole Lyn. 2017. "You Won't Believe How Much Parents Are Now Spending on Their Kids' Birthday Parties." MarketWatch. MarketWatch.com /story/you-wont-believe-how-much-money-parents-are-now-spending-on -their-kids-birthday-parties-2017-07-17-1088523.

Plastic Oceans. 2014. "The Facts." PlasticOceans.org/the-facts.

Platform for Accelerating the Circular Economy. 2019. "A New Circular Vision for Electronics: Time for a Global Reboot." World Economic Forum. www3.WEForum.org/docs/WEF_A_New_Circular_Vision_for_Electronics.pdf.

Platt, Brenda, James McSweeney, and Jenn Davis. 2014. "Growing Local Fertility: A Guide to Community Composting." Institute for Local Self-Reliance. ILSR.org/wp-content/uploads/2014/07/growing-local-fertility.pdf.

Postman, Andrew. 2016. "9 Tricks That Save Tons of Water." Natural Resources Defense Council. NRDC.org/stories/9-tricks-save-tons-water.

Reuse This Bag. 2017. "25 Reasons to Use Reusable Grocery Bags (Updated)." ReuseThisBag.com/articles/25-reasons-to-go-reusable.

Sagon, Candy. 2018. "These Simple Tips for Storing Fruits and Vegetables Will Help You Keep Them Fresh Longer." Science Alert. ScienceAlert.com/how -to-store-10-fruit-and-vegetable-to-make-them-last-longer.

Saplakoglu, Yasemin. 2018. "Scientists Warn BPA-Free Plastic May Not Be Safe." Live Science. LiveScience.com/63592-bpa-free-plastic -dangers.html.

Sarantis, Heather. 2002. "Business Guide to Paper Reduction." ForestEthics. Tufts University. Sustainability.Tufts.edu/wp-content/uploads/Business GuidetoPaperReduction.pdf.

Scheer, Roddy and D. Moss. 2011. "EarthTalk: Cleaning Products Aren't Regulated by the FDA." *The Journal Times.* JournalTimes.com/lifestyles /relationships-and-special-occasions/earthtalk-cleaning-products-arent-regulated-by-the-fda/article_c3fcc038-68a6-11e0-bb3a-001cc4c002e0.html.

Science Daily. 2008. "Toxic Chemicals Found in Common Scented Laundry Products, Air Fresheners." University of Washington. ScienceDaily.com /releases/2008/07/080723134438.htm.

Shrier, Carrie. 2016. "The Value of Open-Ended Play." Michigan State University Extension. Canr.MSU.edu/news/the_value_of_open_ended_play.

Sleep Advisor. 2020. "Toxic Materials in Foam Mattresses? Are We Safe?" SleepAdvisor.org/toxic-materials-in-foam-mattresses.

Soul Fire Farm. 2020. "Online Learning." SoulFireFarm.org/food-sovereignty -education/online-learning.

Sustainable Pulse. 2015. "GM Crops Now Banned in 39 Countries Worldwide." SustainablePulse.com/2015/10/22/gm-crops-now-banned-in-36-countries -worldwide-sustainable-pulse-research/#.Xs_cxC2ZPBI.

Sutton, Rebecca. 2011. "Don't Get Slimed. Skip the Fabric Softener." Environmental Working Group. EWG.org/enviroblog/2011/11/dont-get-slimed-skip -fabric-softener.

Tapp Water. 2019. "How to Filter and Remove Microplastics from Tap Water." TappWater.co/us/how-to-filter-and-remove-microplastics-2/.

Tenenbaum, Laura. 2019. "Plastic Cutlery is Terrible for the Environment and We Don't Need to Have It Delivered." *Forbes.* Forbes.com/sites/lauratenenbaum /2019/07/16/plastic-cutlery-is-terrible-for-the-environment-and-we-dont -need-to-have-it-delivered/#328f09524019.

The World Counts. 2020a. "Electronic Revolution = E-Waste." TheWorldCounts .com/stories/Electronic-Waste-Facts.

The World Counts. 2020b. "Paper Waste Facts." TheWorldCounts.com/stories /Paper-Waste-Facts.

Thompson, Andrea. 2014. "Major Greenhouse Gas Reductions Needed by 2050: IPCC." Climate Central. ClimateCentral.org/news/major-greenhouse -gas-reductions-needed-to-curtail-climate-change-ipcc-17300.

U.S. Environmental Protection Agency (EPA). 1990. *Environmental Consumer's Handbook.*

———. 2014. "Advancing Sustainable Materials Management: *2014 Fact Sheet:* Assessing Trends in Material Generation, Recycling, Composting, Combustion with Energy Recovery and Landfilling in the United States." EPA.gov /sites/production/files/2016-11/documents/2014_smmfactsheet_508.pdf.

———. 2018. "Indoor Air Quality." EPA.gov/report-environment/indoor -air-quality.

———. 2019. "Recycling Basics." EPA.gov/recycle/recycling-basics.

U.S. Food & Drug Administration. n.d. "FDA Authority Over Cosmetics: How Cosmetics Are Not FDA-Approved, But Are FDA-Regulated." FDA.gov /cosmetics/cosmetics-laws-regulations/fda-authority-over-cosmetics-how -cosmetics-are-not-fda-approved-are-fda-regulated.

Valkenburg, Patti, and Moniek Buijzen. 2005. "Identifying Determinants of Young Children's Brand Awareness: Television, Parents, and Peers." *Journal of Applied Developmental Psychology.* ScienceDirect.com/science/article/pii /S0193397305000213.

Walia, Arjun. 2014. "10 Scientific Studies Proving GMOs Can Be Harmful to Human Health." Collective Evolution. Collective-Evolution.com/2014/04/08/10 -scientific-studies-proving-gmos-can-be-harmful-to-human-health.

Warner, Jennifer. 2012. "Is That 'New Car Smell' Toxic?" WebMD. WebMD.com /men/news/20120215/is-that-new-car-smell-toxic#1.

West, Larry. 2019. "How to Stop Receiving Junk Mail." ThoughtCo. ThoughtCo .com/how-to-stop-receiving-junk-mail-1203945.

Zero Waste International Alliance. 2018. "Zero Waste Definition." ZWIA.org /zero-waste-definition.

Index

Acknowledgments

First, my gratitude goes to my daughter Helena, who patiently put up with my hours of work and took on extra chores during the writing period. You're the best! I love you! I'd also like to thank Jeremiah Wallack for his knowledge of all things sustainable and his eagerness to brainstorm and share ideas. Thanks to my editors, Vanessa Ta and Lori Handelman, the alchemists who polished my rough draft into this shining treasure trove of ideas you hold in your hands. Thanks to my puppy S'Barkle. And finally, my thanks to the earth, the natural world that we're a part of and could not exist without.

About the Author

 Rebecca Grace Andrews has a master of arts degree in liberal studies focused on ecopsychology and a master of science degree in herbalism. She's on a lifelong journey to reduce her waste and bring healing to the earth and her inhabitants. Rebecca offers consultations, online classes, and speaking engagements through her business Wild Wellness at RebeccaGraceAndrews. com. She also works as a professor of wellness. In her free time, you can find Rebecca wandering the mountain she calls home, gardening, and hanging out with her fur babies and the-world's-best-unschooled-15-year-old. Rebecca's latest pursuit is an MFA in fine art photography.